ACCLAIM FOR MONDAY MORNING MESSAGES

"The weekly boosts that are found in *Monday Morning Messages* are tremendously engaging, motivating, and often entertaining. What a great idea to provide needed edifying fuel for the upcoming week. Many thousands around the world already think so. This is tested and effective."

—DR. STEPHEN R. COVEY, author
The 7 Habits of Highly Effective People and
The 8th Habit: From Effectiveness to Greatness

"...The principles each message describes helps you to achieve your goals, personal and professional, in a nearly seamless way."

—KEN BLANCHARD, co-author
The One Minute Manager™ and *The Secret*

"For those who dream of building a legacy, making an impact, and exploring all the world has to offer, you're in luck. Few people have had the range of life experience that Bruce Rector has had as World Leader for the largest young professional organization on the planet. In *Monday Morning Messages,* Bruce is both the tour guide and professional mentor that we all dream of, guiding readers through an unforgettable whirlwind trip around the globe."

—JENNIFER KUSHELL, author of
The New York Times bestseller, *Secrets of the Young & Successful: How to Get Everything You Want, Without Waiting a Lifetime*

Monday Morning Messages

Teaching, Inspiring and Motivating to Lead

Bruce A. Rector

XEPHOR
PRESS

XEPHOR
P R E S S

Xephor Press
3 Holly Hill Lane
Katonah, NY 10536
USA
www.xephorpress.com
1-914-232-6708

First printing

ISBN 0-9752638-3-8

Printed and bound in the United States of America.

TABLE OF CONTENTS

III. *Social Awareness*

IV. *Relationship Management*

INTRODUCTION

When the ancients said a work well-begun was half done, they meant to impress the importance of always making a good beginning.

— POLYBIUS

With three minutes remaining in the first half of a football game, my friend Kevin and I, young student athletic trainer assistants, left the playing field to prepare the locker room for the halftime team meeting. Our team, the University of Kentucky, was visiting the home stadium of Clemson University in South Carolina. Over 84,000 screaming Clemson fans were in attendance. The noise generated by the large partisan crowd was deafening, and our team desperately needed to retreat to a quiet locker room to think and refocus before beginning the second half.

Our first task was to move a table from inside the locker room to just outside the door, so we could place water and sports drinks on it. But right after we moved the table through the door, we felt a strong gust of wind and heard the door slam shut behind us. "Do you have the key?" asked Kevin.

"No," I answered.

Kevin had left our team's only key inside the room. We had

locked ourselves and the team out! If we didn't find another way to get back in right away the team would not have a quiet locker room in which to meet during halftime.

Luckily for us, in his ensuing frantic search for help, Kevin met a security guard who had an extra key to the door. He let us into the locker room, just as the horn sounded signaling the end of the first half and seconds before the team ran off the field. For me, that was one of the most stressful moments of my life. I knew how important it was for the coach to gather team members in a quiet place to focus before they went back to the field to compete. Making team members think and reflect one last time before they go forth into an environment full of emotion, hard work, and multiple distractions is critical for any coach.

In my roles outside sports, as a lawyer, university professor, and leader of a 200,000-member worldwide organization, I have learned that people who want to be successful in any endeavor should prepare for their work week much like sports teams prepare to enter the stadium for a big game. For many people, their big game begins each week on Monday morning. After a weekend of rest, relaxation, and reenergizing they prepare to re-enter their office, sales territory, or workplace to make their dreams come true.

Effective leaders and successful people need to be inspired to enter the work week with the same focus and attention to strategy as the members of a team in the locker room. This book will help people who want to be more competitive in life and more productive each week, regardless of whether their goals are social, economic, political, or spiritual.

The messages you will read in this book have been tested and proven to be effective. For more than seven years, they have been refined in response to feedback and conversations with leaders from around the world. I began writing these Monday Morning Messages in 1997, as part of a strategy to teach, inspire, and motivate a team of seven young leaders and entrepreneurs in Europe. They were so moved by the messages that they soon began sharing them with others. Today the mailing list for the electronic version of Monday Morning Messages has grown to become a community of thousands of business, government, and community leaders in more than one hundred countries.

After writing these messages and working with thousands of leaders around the globe, I am convinced that no half-day period of the work week is more important than Monday morning. The events on Monday morning and how we react to them can either destroy our energy, enthusiasm, and productivity for the entire week or provide an uplifting foundation for great accomplishments. It is important that we enter our respective "stadium" each Monday morning focused and ready to perform at the highest level possible. These messages will help you to do just that.

The weekly messages you'll find in this book have impacted people around the world in a way that I never imagined. I have been amazed at the strong reactions from readers. They have told me that the messages have given them more confidence as they enter the work week, more courage to deal with difficult problems, and more hope to make their lifelong dreams come true.

Perhaps the strong positive reaction I have received to the messages is due, at least in part, to the speed and volume with which information now moves and the new challenges that increased flow places on individuals. Although people today may not work longer than a decade ago, technology now allows us to process and do more within a shorter amount of time. This increased technology pressure can leave us feeling more overwhelmed and emotionally "burned-out" than ever before.

The speed at which things move today also means that Monday mornings have often become more stressful and intense. Problems can develop faster over the weekend, and the challenges hitting an individual on Monday morning seem to be getting greater and greater. When I ask an audience, "What is your favorite day of the week?" Monday rarely gets any votes. Monday is so seldom selected that I once asked a seminar participant in Barcelona, Spain, why he had voted for Monday. He responded that he worked Tuesday through Sunday and Monday was his only "off" day!

In this book, I share fifty-two messages with you, a different one to be read every Monday morning for one year. Each message describes a specific strategy. If remembered and applied in your daily life, each strategy will increase your chance of success. I have developed these strategies through my personal experience of leading an international organization and exchanging ideas with thousands of other successful leaders around the world.

The ideas expressed in these messages are simple but, if read carefully and thoughtfully, can be effective and powerful. Read the selected message at the beginning of each week, and then write down and place the quote for the week—found at the end of each chapter—somewhere where you will see it often each day (on your bathroom mirror, by your telephone, on your office calendar). You will experience better Monday mornings, more productive work weeks, and a more successful year.

One of my favorite quotations is by James M. Barrie: "The life of every man is a diary in which he means to write one story, and writes another, and his humblest hour is when he compares the volume as it is written with what he vowed to make it." It is simply not enough to have great goals, high objectives, and exciting dreams. You must have a clear strategy and be effective and focused on that strategy every week. It is important that you dream big dreams for your life and your business, but unless you stay focused on your strategy, despite all the distractions during the competition, the river of life will carry you far downstream. You will realize you have missed your target only when it is too late to do anything to change the outcome.

If you read these messages thoughtfully and consider them carefully, they will prepare you each week to enter your "stadium." They will help you grow, achieve greater success, live a more fulfilling life, and become a more effective leader.

I. Self-Awareness

Act Without Hesitation

*The line between failure and success is so fine
that we scarcely know when we pass it—
so fine that we often are on the line and
we do not know it.*
— RALPH WALDO EMERSON

*For if the trumpet give an uncertain sound,
who shall prepare himself to the battle?*
— I CORINTHIANS 14:8

As my host, Bent, started the car to drive me to the airport, we both thought I had plenty of time to catch my flight. But that began to change as we pulled away from the hotel and reached the end of the short street. Bent had arranged my ticket for the evening flight from Copenhagen to Aalborg,

3

Denmark. I wasn't really sure what time the flight was to depart, but when Bent looked to our left and saw a long line of cars, he said, "Oh," shook his head and, without pausing, turned the car right and headed in the opposite direction.

Since Bent had reserved the ticket, I wasn't really sure what time my flight was scheduled to depart. The speed, purpose, and focus with which Bent weaved the car through the streets of Copenhagen told me that something was going on, but being the strong and silent type, he made no mention of any concerns. He showed little emotion or anxiety when other cars or traffic lights were impeding our progress.

When we reached the freeway, Bent calmly pushed down so hard on the accelerator, that I thought it was going to go right through the floor. The dashboard shook harder and harder as our speed increased. I could feel the forces of gravity against my face as Bent challenged the capability of the engine.

When we arrived at the airport, there were no open parking spots, with the exception of one with a sign above it that read, "Reserved for Rental Car #34." Bent said, "This will have to do," and, without hesitation, turned the car into the open spot.

Once inside the airport terminal, we waited in line for the airline ticket clerk to greet us. A video monitor positioned a meter or so above her head showed the status of the Aalborg flight as "boarding." Then after a few minutes, the listed status changed from "boarding" to "closed." Seeing this, Bent calmly went to the front of the line, interrupted the airline clerk's conversation with a customer, and secured my documents to board the plane. He then turned, handed the papers to me, and said firmly, "Bruce, take this boarding pass and run to the airplane as fast as you possibly can." Without hesitation, I did just as Bent asked. I cleared the metal detector, sped through the gate control, sprinted across the tarmac, quickly climbed the steps to the plane, and took my seat only a few seconds before they closed the airplane door. I made my flight to Aalborg with only seconds to spare.

Had Bent or I hesitated for even a second from the time we left the hotel, I would have missed the flight. This small margin for error was similar to the razor-thin line that separates success and failure in business, government, and community endeavors, large and small. Even the slightest hesitation in pursuing a goal or an opportunity can change the results in a dramatic way. Great leaders understand this and, once they make decisions, they always act upon them without hesitation.

Once you make a decision, how often do you look over your shoulder at the alternatives you left behind? Do you move yourself and your team forward with confidence and conviction, or do you occasionally vacillate, doubting the wisdom of the path you've chosen? Do you motivate your team to follow you with a strong and clear voice or with one that reflects your own uncertainty, fears, and apprehensions about the road ahead?

This week, understand that the line between success and failure in our increasingly competitive world is so thin that nothing but an entirely focused effort will yield the results you desire. Sound your trumpet with a clear and strong sound and in a way that will cause your team to follow you into even the fiercest competition. Begin regularly moving forward, acting on your decisions with the power of conviction.

Even the slightest hesitation in pursuing a goal or an opportunity can change the results in a dramatic way. Great leaders understand this and, once they make decisions, they always act upon them without hesitation.

Know Where You Are

*Ninety percent of the world's woes come from
people not knowing themselves, their
abilities, their frailties, and even their real
virtues. Most of us go all the way through life
as complete strangers to ourselves—so how
can we know anyone else.*
— SYDNEY J. HARRIS

It was a cold and windy morning as I jogged
through a park in Tallinn, Estonia. As I reached the end of the
soft jogging trail, I had to choose whether to stay in the park and
turn back in the direction from which I came or to keep going
straight. I chose to go straight and to proceed into the "Old Town"
with its medieval network of buildings and cobblestone streets. It
was a rare opportunity for me to jog through a town that looks

today much as it did nearly 700 years ago.

Jogging past the Tallinn Town Hall, built in 1322, I was capti-vated by the charm and history of my surroundings, but my en-joyment was not helping to keep me warm. When I spotted a few falling snowflakes, I decided to head back to my hotel. Unfortu-nately, I had been enjoying the view of the city so much that I really wasn't sure where I was and how to get to my hotel from here. I thought about stopping and asking for directions, but be-ing a man, the thought quickly passed and I kept running. I was confident that if I just kept running, I would find the right way.

I passed through the gates of the Old Town walls and ran along a street that looked familiar. I thought I was finally headed in the right direction, but after a few minutes, it began to look unfamiliar. More and more snow kept falling and the wind be-came stronger and colder, but rather than stop and ask for direc-tions, I kept running.

After a lot of running along streets that at first looked familiar and then unfamiliar, I did something difficult for most men to do: I finally stopped running and asked someone for directions. Then, having a clear understanding of where I was, I began running again and only a few minutes later, I reached the hotel.

Had I not stopped to ask for directions, I might still be run-ning through the streets of Tallinn today. Although I knew where I wanted to go, I wasn't sure where I was. Without knowing both, there was little hope that I was ever going to reach my intended destination.

Outstanding leaders maintain a good grasp of where they are as well as where they want to be. They have a thorough under-standing of where they are with respect to their abilities, their frailties, and their values, and they reflect on them before they begin each day. They know that, without having a firm foundation of strongly held virtues and self-awareness, they will never reach their intended destinations. Regardless of how fast or long they run.

Are you just jogging through life, captivated by your surroundings, and unknowingly losing your sense of where you are? How often do you pause in the frantic efforts to reach your goals, to collect your thoughts, evaluate who you are as a person, and consider if you are running in the right direction?

Take a few moments each day of this week to reflect upon where you are as a leader, a parent, or a person, and compare that to where you want to be. Evaluate your abilities, your frailties, and your virtues to better understand others by first knowing yourself. Stop running through life long enough to make sure you know where you are and ask for directions and input from others. Clearly understand where you are as well as where you want to be, and then achieve your goals by closing the gap between the two.

Outstanding leaders maintain a good grasp of where they are as well as where they want to be. They know that, without having a firm foundation of strongly held virtues and self-awareness, they will never reach their intended destinations. Regardless of how fast or long they run.

Add a Personal Touch

A man's greatest enemies are his own apathy and stubbornness.
— FRANK TYGER

Common sense is the knack of seeing things as they are, and doing things as they ought to be done.
— HARRIET BEECHER STOWE

I suspected trouble when the airline gate attendant called me to the counter. I knew the plane only had thirty or so seats and no first or business class, so she would not be offering me an upgrade. I approached her expecting to receive bad news.

"Mr. Rector, you are the only passenger on this flight so I'll need you to go through a security check," said the gate attendant. I have flown in airplanes many times over the past couple of years, but I've never been the only passenger in the plane. I had no idea of what to expect when I got on board.

Entering the airplane, I met the flight attendant, Amy. Amy greeted me with a smile, helped me put my bags into the overhead compartment, sat down next to me, and said, "I've never had a flight with only one passenger so I think I'll just go over the flight safety information here rather than use the microphone up front." Amy showed me where the oxygen masks were located, but rather than following her normal script she engaged me in conversation as she went along. Then she closed by saying, "You're the only passenger on the plane, so rather than following the normal routine, anytime you want something to eat or drink, just let me know. More or less just make yourself at home."

Throughout the flight, I thought about how many flight attendants would have made the effort to personalize my flight the way Amy did, even though I was the only passenger. Flight attendants are trained to follow the same routine over and over so that they will be more efficient. But often flight attendants sound and look uncommonly stilted as they recite the memorized preflight safety information, serve beverages, and perform their duties.

Like flight attendants, organizing our own daily lives with systems and routines can help us to be more efficient and productive, but in doing so, we risk becoming so set in those routines that they make us apathetic and stubborn. We can begin to act more like robots than people, and that apathy and stubbornness can become our greatest enemy. We can become blind to the way things really are and, as a result, do not always do things as they ought to be done.

What routines, systems, and habits have you developed that may cause you to be apathetic and stubborn? In what ways do you make an effort to personalize what you do even though having a set way of doing things is necessary to allow you to be efficient and productive? Despite the busy and frantic schedule you may have, how do you remind yourself to see things the way they are and to do things as they ought to be done?

This week, remember that routines should never be used as an excuse to disregard common sense. Don't let apathy and stubbornness stop you from seeing things the way they are and deviating from systems when it's appropriate to do so. Despite your usual way of doing things, add a personal touch to your work when common sense tells you it is the way things ought to be done.

Organizing our own daily lives with systems and routines can help us to be more efficient and productive, but in doing so, we risk becoming so set in those routines that they make us apathetic and stubborn.

Stand Back

*Live your life each day as you would climb a
mountain. An occasional glance toward the
summit keeps the goal in mind, but many
beautiful scenes are to be observed from each
new vantage point. Climb slowly, steadily,
enjoying each passing moment; and the view
from the summit will serve as a fitting climax
for the journey.*
— HAROLD V. MELCHERT

Standing close to the walls of the Taj Mahal in
India, one is fascinated with the incredible detail of the work-
manship. Set into the white marble walls are intricate floral, geo-
metric, and calligraphy stone inlays. The magnificence of the *pietra
dura,* whereby thin sections of precisely carved hard and semi-
hard gemstones are laid in sockets specially prepared in the surface of the marble, is one of the reasons why the structure is

15

identified as a man-made wonder of the world. The impressive decorative details that can only be appreciated by standing very close to the structure make it easier to understand why centuries ago it took twenty-two years to complete.

But as spectacular as the detailed carvings are on the Taj Mahal, to capture the real beauty of it, you have to stand one hundred meters or more away from the structure. When looking at the Taj from across the impressive garden that leads to it from the main gateway, the building has an almost surreal appearance. The effect of the daylight upon the Taj's white marble and the symmetry of the structure produce an awe-inspiring visual effect like no other in the world.

Much like appreciating the Taj Mahal, we also must stand back from the details of our frenetic daily schedules in order to see the true beauty of life. Although the challenge of climbing to the top and reaching our goals can be exciting and requires our concentration on the details, we must never forget to "stand back" from time to time and enjoy the view on the way up.

Are you so busy giving attention to the details of chasing your goals and dreams that you are not stopping from time to time to enjoy the beauty of the climb? Do you "stand back" occasionally to focus on the overall good in your life, or do you focus too narrowly upon the relatively few things that do not go right? Are you taking time to enjoy and embrace the many simple, but too often unnoticed, beautiful scenes that play out in your life each day?

Take some time this week to "stand back" from the details of your life. Keep in mind that each new day brings a new opportunity to see yourself and the world around you in a new way. As you go throughout your daily routine, never lose sight of the big picture and pause occasionally to enjoy the many beautiful scenes along the way.

Although the challenge of climbing to the top and reaching our goals can be exciting and requires our concentration on the details, we must never forget to "stand back" from time to time and enjoy the view on the way up.

Be
Remembered

*If you would succeed in life, it is of first
importance that your individuality, your
independence, your determination
be trained that you not be lost in the crowd.*
— ORISON S. MARDEN

Having traveled to almost fifty countries in one year recently, you can understand that checking into a hotel is usually not a big event for me. But of the hundreds of very nice hotels I stayed in over the years, one small hotel in Switzerland recently stood out.

When I arrived at the reception desk of the hotel, a staff member of the hotel greeted me with a smile and gathered from me the usual information needed for check-in. As she handed the room key to me, she surprised me by saying, "Mr. Rector, there is currently a feather pillow on your bed, but if you prefer another pillow from this menu, then please let us know and we will bring it to you." She then handed me the hotel's "Pillow Menu." Thirteen pillows were listed on the menu along with a short description of each one.

Although I had never been offered a "Pillow Menu" before, I didn't request a pillow different from the one that was already on my bed. My guess is that most guests of the hotel don't request a different pillow from the menu either. But the offer of the hotel was a gesture that I won't ever forget. It was a way for the hotel to get my attention and cause me to notice the quality exhibited in other aspects of the hotel. This hotel's "Pillow Menu" was a unique way for it to stand out from the many very nice hotels in the area and to try to avoid being lost in the crowd.

Much like the "Pillow Menu" of that hotel in Switzerland, successful business, government, and community leaders also find creative ways for those they work with to remember them and to notice the quality of their work. They realize that simply being a good leader is not enough. They understand that they must continually be looking for ways to rise above mediocrity and complacency. They understand that getting people to notice and remember them is just as important for success as talent and hard work.

What are you doing to set yourself apart from the crowd of other leaders so that people will notice your work and remember you? How is the team or organization that you lead surprising the customers, clients, or members that you serve in a way that causes them to notice the quality of your work and to think of you as the best?

This week, focus on training your individuality, independence, and determination in a way that they will keep you from being lost in the crowd. In every aspect of your life and your work, be aware that the good is always the enemy of the best. Then find new and unique ways to cause those around you to notice and to remember the quality of your work.

Simply being a good leader is not enough. Getting people to notice and remember you is just as important for success as talent and hard work.

Use a
Quiet Spot

*It is an experiment worth trying to be alone
and to be quiet for a brief period every day.
Under city conditions it may be difficult to
carry out, but most of us could do it
if we tried.*
— ROBERT J. MCCRACKEN

My friend Melissa sent a message to me. In the message, she pointed out a place near the downtown area of our city that I did not know about. It is located on a street that does not get much traffic or attention and is hidden from view by trees and a fire station. With an open green lawn and a nice brick pathway, it is only a few minutes walk from my office, and it is a nice place to stop during the day to relieve some stress and to think. Melissa wrote, "I thought you might like to know of a quiet

23

spot to enjoy from time to time during your busy days."

Most business, government, and community leaders rarely consider the importance of building a quiet moment or two into their daily schedules. But nothing can be more effective in helping you to be creative than to stop the rapid pace of your schedule for at least a brief period each day to think and reflect. Innovation and success in both your personal life and for your team require you to do more than just aim and fire as rapidly as you can all day long. To achieve greatness in whatever you pursue, you must pause occasionally to challenge yourself and your ideas, not in the bustle of a busy office, but in a quiet environment where you can truly reflect.

Are the stress and discontent that naturally build up during your day, preventing you from performing your best? When was the last time you scheduled some quiet moments into your daily schedule? Where can you quickly slip away when you need to pause, reflect, and consider your ideas without being distracted?

This week, find a quiet spot that you can go to each day in order to be alone and to think. Great thoughts will not come to you while you are in a frantic, get-through-the-work-as-fast-as-I-can routine. Include some silence in your daily work schedule and allow your soul to be visited from on high so that you can truly give your most inspired and best performance.

To achieve greatness in whatever you pursue,
you must pause occasionally to challenge
yourself and your ideas, not in the bustle of a
busy office, but in a quiet environment where
you can truly reflect.

Challenge Your Assumptions

*A long habit of not thinking a thing wrong
gives it the superficial appearance of being
right, and raises at first a formidable outcry
in defense of custom. But the tumult soon
subsides. Time wins more converts
than reason.*

— THOMAS PAINE

After a long trip from my home to the Dominican Republic, I was exhausted and had no trouble falling into a deep sleep soon after reaching my hotel room. But at 12:45 a.m. something awakened me. It felt as though my bed was moving back and forth, and I could hear the windows, doors, and lamps rattling. I also heard the footsteps of someone running down the hallway just outside my room.

At first, I thought the noise must have been coming from a party in the room next to me. But lying in bed in the darkness, I eventually decided that someone was trying to break into my room. I remained very still and quiet hoping they would go away. The bed stopped shaking and I soon fell asleep again.

The next morning, I looked at the thick concrete walls of my room. No man could have made these walls move enough to cause my bed to shake. I again assumed that it had been a party that had awakened me, but now I believed I must have only dreamt that my bed had been shaking.

On the way to breakfast, I stopped by the front desk of the hotel to complain about the noise from the night before. "It must have been the earthquake that awakened you," said the hotel clerk. My bed really had been shaking that previous night. The Dominican Republic had experienced an earthquake, which measured 6.5 on the Richter Scale—the strongest one in that country in more than forty years.

I had never felt an earthquake before, and I based my interpretation of what was happening that night on my own past personal experience. Unfortunately, I could not find the correct explanation, because my past experience led me to assume that the cause of the disturbance was man-made.

Often leaders and organizations are also blinded by their own wrong assumptions when based solely upon past personal experience. With that limited perspective, they assume that what has worked so well for them in the past will work best today. They cannot see the best strategies for achieving success in the future because of rigid basic assumptions that have been formed by past successes, traditions, and customs.

Outstanding leaders understand the limiting effect of assumptions. They work hard to keep their minds open to new strategies, practices, and systems, regardless of their own past personal experiences. They continually challenge their own habits, traditions, and customs to ensure that what worked well yesterday still works today.

This week, begin challenging your basic assumptions on a regular basis. Begin maintaining only those habits and traditions that still make sense and abandon those that do not. Avoid defending custom without first challenging the thinking that supports it and making sure that it is still relevant to helping you to enjoy a fulfilling life and enabling your team or organization to achieve success today.

Outstanding leaders understand the limiting effect of assumptions. They work hard to keep their minds open to new strategies, practices, and systems, regardless of their own past personal experiences. They continually challenge their own habits, traditions, and customs to ensure that what worked well yesterday still works today.

Look for a More Beautiful View

It is right to be contented with what we have,
never with what we are.
— JAMES MACKINTOSH

Stepping into the car in Northern Italy, we began our journey toward Graz, Austria. It was a beautiful day with warm temperatures and a clear blue sky.

As we began traveling, we had spectacular views of the mountains and surrounding valleys. Each view was breathtaking and seemed to be the best view possible. But as we climbed and went twisting and turning further into the Alps, the next view would be even more fantastic. With the sun setting, the mountains looked even more beautiful, and the seemingly perfect views kept getting better and better.

Later that evening in Graz, I was reminded that Graz is the

hometown of Arnold Schwarzenegger, whose life had taken twists and turns similar to those we experienced during our trip through Northern Italy and Austria. Born into a family of rather modest means, Schwarzenegger had first achieved success as a bodybuilder in Austria and America. Rather than resting upon his great success in the fitness industry, he pushed himself out of his comfort zone to become an actor in motion pictures. A huge financial success in Hollywood, he then went around another turn and gained an even more beautiful view by being elected governor of California, the most populous state in the United States.

Outstanding leaders and successful people have an insatiable curiosity for new challenges. They are content with what they have but never with what they are. They constantly look for new ways and opportunities to achieve a more beautiful view of life, even though their current situation might appear as good as it gets.

Are you too content with what you are and what you have already done? Do you push yourself enough to get out of your comfort zone and to experience new physical, mental, and spiritual challenges? Are you missing even more spectacular views of life because you have convinced yourself that your circumstances cannot get any better?

Pause this week to appreciate what you have already accomplished, but also begin looking for your next challenge. Learn to always look for new opportunities, even when things seem to be as good as it gets. Push yourself to think of new opportunities. Continue your travel on the road of life, searching for a more beautiful view, even though the one you are enjoying now may seem to be the best possible.

*Outstanding leaders and successful people have
an insatiable curiosity for new challenges.
They are content with what they have but never
with what they are.*

Embrace the New Day

*I have always been delighted at the prospect
of a new day, a fresh try, one more start, with
perhaps a little bit of magic waiting behind
the morning.*

— J.B. Priestly

As I have grown older, a lot has changed with regard to the way I start each day. For instance, my muscles ache more in the mornings than they used to. And it seems to take a little longer to get my body and mind warmed up to start the day.

But once I am ready for the day, my maturity has added a new perspective to my attitude. With a growing appreciation that my heart is still beating, after having known more and more men and women younger than I whose lives have ended, I now see each day as more of an opportunity and a fresh start than ever before.

And I have become more impressed with people like the successful businessman I once met, who remarked that at age sixty, he was getting ready to start his third career. At an age when others would be ready to retire for good, this man was ready to try one more start.

Each day of this week, think about how you are approaching the prospect of a new day. Treat each day as an opportunity, a fresh start, and a chance for a new beginning. Begin every day looking for that "bit of magic" that might be waiting for you somewhere behind the morning.

At age sixty, he was getting ready to start his third career. At an age when others would be ready to retire for good, this man was ready to try one more start.

Pay the Price

*Happy are those who dream dreams and are
ready to pay the price to make them
come true.*
— LEON J. SUENENS

My three-year-old son, Trevor, was ahead of the pack of other children on a soccer field in Lexington, Kentucky, as the ball popped out from a pack of players and came his way. Seizing the opportunity, he chased the ball down the field and then kicked it into the open goal. In his first game ever and as the youngest soccer player on his team, Trevor had scored a goal and his team celebrated with him.

Does this sound like a perfect story to you? Well almost. Missing from the celebration of this major achievement was his father. While my son was scoring his first goal in his first soccer game, I was 7,000 miles away, sleeping in my hotel room in Fukui, Japan. The next morning, I was going to present my remarks to the National Convention of Japan Junior Chamber. Ten thousand people would be in attendance, including Prince and Princess Hitachinomiya of Japan. It was a once-in-a-lifetime experience for me, but I was paying a heavy personal price by missing my son's first game.

Outstanding leaders must be willing to make sacrifices to make their dreams come true. They know that it is not enough to just dream dreams; they must be willing to also pay the price. The sacrifice I made in missing an important event such as my son's first soccer goal was not one that I would choose to make very often. But it brought my attention to the many trivial pursuits that you and I could give up to "pay the price" each day and make our dreams come true.

Do you "pay the price" by pausing at the beginning of your busy day to spend time focusing on your dreams and goals? Are you willing to "pay the price" by forgoing even simple pleasures such as watching television or reading the newspaper to free up more time each day to chase your dreams? Would you be willing to "pay the price" by sacrificing nonessential aspects of your lifestyle to save the money needed to start up your dream endeavor?

This week, question your resolve to "pay the price" to make your dreams come true. Focus on what additional energy, time, and resources you can pull away from other activities in order to pursue your dreams. Look for simple sacrifices that you could be making in your daily life to increase your chances of success. Choose to be happy by dreaming dreams and then being ready to pay the price to make those dreams come true.

Outstanding leaders know that it is not enough to just dream dreams; they must be willing to also pay the price.

Control Your Anger

*Consider how much more you often suffer
from your anger and grief,
than from those very things for which
you are angry and grieved.*
— MARCUS AURELIUS ANTONIUS

Air travel today can be a frustrating experience. In addition to contending with added security regulations and procedures, lost or misplaced luggage is still common on many airlines.

Although I arrived at the airport in Hamburg, Germany, on a trip from my home in Kentucky in September, 2002, my luggage did not. Having traveled on hundreds of flights I have had this happen before. So I had no problem getting by with the items in my carry-on bag for four days until I finally collected my luggage

39

as I was checking in at the same airport to return to the United States. I've learned that getting angry about lost luggage doesn't help me to get it any faster or prevent it from happening again, so I just plan for that possibility and work around it.

Years ago, I might have had a different response to the loss of my luggage. I probably would have looked like a lot of the people I saw around me at the Hamburg and Paris airports during my return home. The airline on which I was flying was canceling flights and rescheduling the trips of many passengers because its pilots were on strike. Some of these passengers were so angry, and their faces so red, that they looked like their scalps might blow right off their heads at any moment. Other than increasing their own blood pressure and stress level, their anger was not having much effect.

Today I've learned to stay calm when faced with frustrating situations by asking myself a simple question: What can I do in response to this that will make my situation better? Getting angry is almost never a good answer to that question.

Are you able to recognize the difference between the things you cannot change and those you can? Do you realize that the consequences of your anger may cause you to suffer more than the event that triggered it? Would you be a more effective leader of your team, organization, or family, if you chose to react calmly to unexpected events by asking yourself what you could do to make your situation better rather than getting angry and expecting others to improve things for you?

This week give thought to how you approach those things and events that might cause you to be angry. Try to focus your energy in those situations on the things that you can control rather than those things that you cannot. Consider the energy and effort that you waste with anger, and choose to put that energy and effort to a more productive use.

In frustrating situations, ask yourself a simple question: What can I do in response to this that will make my situation better? Getting angry is almost never a good answer to that question.

Choose the Uncommon Roads

*When a great man has some one object in
view to be achieved in a given time, it may be
absolutely necessary for him to walk out of
all the common roads.*

— EDMUND BURKE

In the movie *Jerry Maguire,* the boss, Jerry
Maguire, assures his employee, Dorothy Boyd, that despite losing
a major client, he will make sure that Boyd still has a job with
him. To that, Boyd, a single mother of a young boy, responds, "I
care about the job, of course, but what I want mostly is to be
inspired."

Most of us spend at least 50 percent of our waking hours

43

Monday through Friday at work. This is a huge portion of our week and added up over a lifetime is a significant percentage of our lives. Despite that, a survey of college-educated employees several years ago by a respected national polling organization showed that 18 percent viewed their job as "mostly just a way to make money" and another 52 percent viewed their job as "meaningful, but not as meaningful as the rest of my life." That's a total of 70 percent that, while at work, would arguably rather be somewhere else.

The survey results confirm to me that we can't count on getting the inspiration we need to excel in our careers and our work without seeking it. If you wait for work to inspire you, it may never happen. And even if you own your own business, if you don't continually try to seek inspiration, you may burn out and your business may begin to struggle.

I have seen and read of successful people who make exposing themselves to inspiration a part of their regular routine in order to stay fresh, creative, and innovative. Rather than being intimidated by other talented people, successful people seek to hire and surround themselves with bright employees and co-workers because they know that these people will inspire them to work harder and smarter.

One of the routine things that I like to do to inspire myself is to spend at least two weeks per year vacationing near the ocean. I get a special feeling when I am by the sea. Some of my most creative thoughts about my future have taken place on walks along the beach.

This week, ask yourself what kinds of activities inspire you the most. Set aside some time in your schedule to engage in these inspirational activities. Clearly, you must do more than just find a job, show up to work, and wait for inspiration to come your way.

When it comes to being inspired at work, you must separate yourself from the 70 percent in the Roper Starch survey who would rather be doing something else. Dedicate yourself to occasionally walking "out of all the common roads" in order to give yourself a chance to be inspired.

If you wait for work to inspire you, it may never happen. And even if you own your own business, if you don't continually try to seek inspiration, you may burn out and your business may begin to struggle.

Enjoy
Receiving

*Each day I try to do three things: I laugh, I
think, and I cry. If you laugh, you think, and
you cry, that's a pretty full day. You do that
seven days a week, and you're gonna have
something special.*

— JIM VALVANO

He struggled from his chair and gingerly
climbed the three steps at the foot of the stage leading to the
podium. When he grabbed the podium to support himself and
faced the crowd, the pain caused by the cancerous tumors throughout his body was evident on his grimacing face. But he pushed
himself through it because he wanted to say a few words in ac-
ceptance of the award that he had just been given.

Jim Valvano, former college basketball coach and television

commentator, had been selected to receive the Arthur Ashe Award at the 1993 ESPY awards in New York City. Present in the audience were many celebrities and some of the greatest athletes in the world. All of them sat in rapt attention as Valvano spoke.

As Valvano gave his remarks, it seemed that with each word he gathered more and more strength. The audience knew that he was losing his fight with cancer. As the television cameras surveyed the crowd, you could see that they were amazed by his courage and effort in light of his physically draining fight with the terminal illness.

Despite the tremendous pain, Jim smiled throughout his remarks. He urged the audience "to enjoy life" and "to be enthusiastic every day." In the several minutes that he was given to talk, Jim made the audience laugh, think, and cry. He enjoyed the moment of receiving the award, and it showed.

As business, government, community, and family leaders, we often place tremendous emphasis on teaching others the value of giving. Giving is important. We only receive the most precious gifts because we are willing to give ourselves.

But Jim Valvano taught the audience that night in New York City that it is as important to know how to receive as it is to know how to give. He reminded them that each morning we receive the gift of a new day. And how we choose to receive that gift makes the difference between whether or not our dreams become a reality.

Valvano told the crowd just before he left the podium that night that "every minute I have left I will thank God for the minute and the moment I have." When he concluded, the crowd rose to a standing ovation. Jim had to be assisted off the stage and back to his chair. He died a few months later.

This week, think about how good you are at receiving the gift of life each day. Approach each day with enthusiasm and throw yourself into what you are doing with all that you have so that each day you laugh, you think, and you cry. Only by doing those three things each day, will you be assured of living a special life.

Jim Valvano taught that it is as important to know how to receive as it is to know how to give. Each morning we receive the gift of a new day. And how we choose to receive that gift makes the difference between whether or not our dreams become a reality.

Turn the Clock to Zero

*The best thing about the future is that it
comes only one day at a time.*
— ABRAHAM LINCOLN

One of my favorite holiday season music CDs
is *Star Bright* by Vanessa Williams (Mercury Records 1996). The
CD not only puts me into the mood for the holidays, but it also
reminds me of the continual need to put the past behind me and
turn the clock to zero as I start each new day.

Vanessa Williams has had remarkable success in music, movies, television, and theatre. She has been honored with many
awards for her work. But her eventual success was not so obvious
to her in 1984.

After becoming the first woman of African descent to win the
Miss America title, Williams resigned from that role during her

reign because of photographs taken of her when she was a teen-ager and that were to be published in *Penthouse* magazine. The twenty-year-old Williams had suddenly gone from the top to the bottom. Because of the sexual nature of the photographs, she lost more than $2 million in endorsement deals and the lead role in a Broadway musical. Perhaps even worse, she had been embarrassed and humiliated before the entire world.

As difficult and depressing as her situation was, Williams de-cided to grow stronger from her experience rather than to be defeated by it. Although it would have been easier and less threat-ening for her to permanently retreat from public life, she recog-nized that she still had the same talents for singing and acting, even though she no longer had respect.

Only a year later, Williams was performing again, by singing backup vocals on two songs for recording artist George Clinton. On those projects she caught the attention of Mercury Records executives, and after a few meetings, they signed her to a record-ing contract. Williams was soon receiving awards and critical ac-claim for her various singing and acting performances.

Presented with Williams' situation many people might have been so overcome by embarrassment, humiliation, and anger that they could not move forward. Rather than trying to leave yester-day behind them and moving forward to take advantage of the opportunities of the new day, they would have focused their en-ergy on blaming others for their circumstances, feeling sorry for themselves, and perhaps even seeking revenge.

Outstanding business, government, community, and family leaders view each morning as a fresh start. They recognize that although the previous day is behind them so are their mistakes. Outstanding leaders have a sense of the extreme importance of tomorrow. They understand that yesterday is over, and they always think of the coming day as being the most important day.

During your life, political foes may try to dredge up your past in an effort to discourage you. Competitors may constantly remind you of yesterday. This week remember that each new day is the most important day because it is your chance to let go of the past and focus on the future. Each day look for a fresh start and a new beginning. Take a moment this and every morning to reflect upon not only the challenges but also the promise and hope of the new day.

Outstanding leaders have a sense of the extreme importance of tomorrow. They understand that yesterday is over, and they always think of the coming day as being the most important day.

II. Self-Management

Adjust the
Little Things

*Life is made up of little things. It is very
rarely that an occasion is offered for doing a
great deal at once. True greatness consists in
being great in little things.*
— CHARLES SIMMONS

It takes only a second. You are driving your car,
and you look away from the road to adjust the radio, respond to
your crying child, or look at something along the roadside. Before you know it, your car has slipped off the edge of the road.
Realizing what you have done, you calmly correct your mistake
and steer the car back to its proper place on the road and continue your journey.

Anyone who has driven a car has had, at some point, an experience like the one described above. And we all know that the safest way to react is to remain calm. Any overreaction or sudden movements of the steering wheel can cause the driver to lose control of the car.

December is the time of the year when I reflect upon the road I have been traveling in the past year and ask myself if I am heading in the direction I want to go. I often find that, during the previous year, my life has slipped a little off the edge of the road. I see that I have neglected some of the things in my life that I am the most passionate about: my faith, my family, my health. I pledge to change my habits in the coming year.

The key to improving this year is to respond as if we were driving a car that has slipped from the edge of the road. I read yesterday that of the one-third of the people that adopt resolutions to change some aspect of their lives for the New Year, only one-third keep them. Many of them fail because they are too ambitious, overreact, and try to change too much, too fast. We are more likely to succeed in creating long-term change in our lives if we react calmly and rationally when we set and endeavor to achieve our goals in the coming year. To improve and get back on track, we must give slow and steady attention to many little things rather than trying to do a great deal at once.

Have you slipped off the edge of the road in the past year? Do you find yourself spending less time in the areas of your life that you are the most passionate about than you were a year ago? Do you have the tendency to overreact by setting extreme goals that you'll likely abandon within a couple of months? Are you ready to calmly pull yourself back on the road by adjusting the little things in your daily routines?

Focus this week on those things that drive your existence and identify ways you can improve them in the coming year. Dedicate yourself to calmly and slowly pulling your life back to where you want it to be. Set clear, measurable, but reasonable goals for making changes in your life. Begin the New Year with the attitude that you are going to make great things happen this year by giving careful attention and adjustments to the many little things that make up life.

We are more likely to succeed in creating long-term change in our lives if we react calmly and rationally when we set and endeavor to achieve our goals in the coming year. To improve and get back on track, we must give slow and steady attention to many little things rather than trying to do a great deal at once.

Confront Your Enemy

From time waste there can be no salvage. It is the easiest of all waste and the hardest to correct because it does not litter the floor.
— HENRY FORD

My time waste enemy awaits me as I enter the door to my home. At sixty-one inches (155 centimeters) wide I cannot overlook it. It stares at me. It beckons me to get comfortable in a chair and to turn it on. It wants to disrupt the activities that I have planned and that would be a more productive use of my time. By projecting American football games, it has the ability to reach deep inside me and stir my testosterone. Hours of watching football on my television seem like minutes, and before I know it, my Saturday or Sunday afternoon has gotten away from me.

Like my interest in watching televised football games, often the greatest time waste enemies are the ones that we fail to recognize or admit. We don't stop to realize how much time we are spending doing them and what better use we could make of the time. For instance, the television is turned on in the average American home for seven hours and forty minutes every day. Yet fewer than half of Americans surveyed in one poll admitted that they spend too much time watching television.

Whether we recognize it or not, we all have a time waste enemy. What is your enemy? Do you spend too much time on the computer and not enough time getting out of your house to meet people? Are you getting so carried away with your work, that you are not spending enough time with your growing children? Has your passion for your favorite hobby become so strong that you really don't know how much time you're spending with it?

This week, keep a detailed diary of each day so that you can see more clearly how you are actually spending your time. Identify your time waste enemy, which is that activity you are spending more time on than you should be if you are going to live a satisfying life and achieve your long-term dreams. Then confront that enemy by developing a strategy to defeat it and eliminate from your life the time waste from which there can be no salvage.

*The television is turned on in the average
American home for seven hours and forty
minutes every day. Yet fewer than half of
Americans surveyed in one poll admitted that
they spend too much time watching television.*

Address
the Cause

*It is a good rule to face difficulties at the time
they arise and not allow them to increase
unacknowledged.*
— EDWARD W. ZIEGLER

I ignored my wisdom teeth as long as I could,
but finally my dentist told me that I had waited too long and they
had to come out. After more than ten years of treating the periodic painful flare-ups, it was time for me to quit treating the symptoms and address the cause. I scheduled the surgery that day and
had them removed a month later.

After the surgery, I experienced some initial discomfort, but
the results have been great. I no longer have the occasional tooth
pain that sometimes affected my energy and effectiveness. It was
worth the time, pain, and money to have the wisdom teeth

removed, and I wish I had done it much sooner. Treating the symptoms over the years rather than dealing with the cause was like putting a fresh coat of paint on a rusting pole or a decaying piece of wood. Covering up and ignoring the real problem allowed me to keep going, but it did not stop the problem from getting worse.

Teams and organizations also can allow problems to grow and worsen because of a reluctance to address tough issues at the time they arise. We have all been participants in meetings where people spend hours debating how to treat the symptoms of a problem but never get around to discussing the cause. To avoid the potential pain of offending or angering someone, they avoid talking about the proverbial "elephant" in the room: the cause of the problem that everyone sees but that no one has the courage to address.

What tough issues are your team members reluctant to face when you meet to discuss challenges or strategy? As a leader, do you have the courage to identify and begin the conversation about the "elephant in the room" when it's hurting your organization to ignore it? Is there any underlying problem in your life that keeps flaring up from time to time, causes you pain or discomfort, and will only get worse until you finally decide to face and resolve it?

This week, begin facing your difficulties at the time they arise rather than letting them increase unacknowledged. Develop the habit of always addressing the real cause rather than just treating the symptoms. Have the courage to discuss the most important issue instead of tiptoeing around "the elephant."

Teams and organizations also can allow problems to grow and worsen because of a reluctance to address tough issues at the time they arise.

Always Give It Your Best

Measure yourself by your best moments, not by your worst. We are too prone to judge ourselves by our moments of despondency and depression. We have all felt the desire, at times, almost victorious desire, to get away from everything and retire into a cottage in the wilderness. But we don't do it, because we are better men and women than we think we are.

— ROBERT JOHNSON

With five seconds remaining in the American high school football game, Jake Porter trotted onto the field. Despite having been born with a disorder known as "Chromosomal Fragile-X," which is the most common cause of mental retardation, Jake had shown up for practice every day for four years. But because of his condition, he had never been in a game for an official play. At the end of his senior, and last, season on the team, Jake's coach, Dave Frantz, wanted that to change.

Earlier in the week, Frantz had called the opposing coach, Derek Dewitt. Frantz explained Jake's condition and told Dewitt that any physical contact with Jake might jeopardize his life. He told DeWitt that if the game were not at stake, he'd like to put Jake in the game for the last play. He asked Dewitt to tell his players not to tackle Jake, and when they handed the ball to him, Jake would immediately drop to his knee to let the remaining time on the clock run out. To reward Jake's loyalty, dedication, and hard work the previous four years, Frantz just wanted to let him have the feel of the ball in his hands during a real game.

With the score at 42-0 in favor of DeWitt's team, only five seconds left, and Jake trotting onto the field, DeWitt met Frantz in the middle of the field and surprised Frantz with a suggestion. "We'll let him score," said DeWitt. Jake had only practiced dropping to his knee, so initially Frantz resisted. But then he finally agreed and instructed his team to hand the ball to Jake and let him run for a touchdown.

When the play began, the other twenty-one players on the field opened the way for Jake to run toward the end zone. Having been handed the ball, Jake was confused at first. He stopped running and turned back to his original starting position for the play. But then with everyone on the field, including the defensive players from the other team, pointing the way, cheering him on, and running step-for-step with him for forty-nine yards (forty-four meters), Jake reached the end zone and scored a touchdown for his team.

Upon seeing Jake's accomplishment, many fans and

players began cheering wildly. Some were so moved that tears ran down their cheeks. Although the play only lasted ten seconds, it will be long remembered by those who saw the seventeen-year-old's persistence rewarded, his dream come true, and his life changed forever.

Life is not easy for any of us. Even if we are born with perfect minds, each person experiences plenty of discouragement and disappointment. Regardless of our level of natural talent, intelligence, and skill, it can be easy to dwell on what is not going right in our lives and to think that giving our best effort won't make any difference. But Jake Porter's story should remind us of the importance of not letting our shortcomings and deficiencies be an excuse to not give life a full effort. Persistent people like Jake, who refuse to use their challenges as an excuse, should inspire us to always do the best we can with what we have.

This week, measure yourself by your best moments, not your worst. Resolve to give your best effort in everything you do regardless of whether you think you are less gifted than your competition. Like Jake Porter, refuse to use your challenges as an excuse and do those things each day that will win you the respect of those around you. Never let moments of despondency and depression, which we all encounter from time to time, cause you to retreat from your dreams. Strive each day to be a better man or woman than you sometimes might think you are.

*Persistent people who refuse to use their
challenges as an excuse should inspire us to
always do the best we can with what we have.*

Prepare and
Anticipate

WEEK 19

*The executive of the future will be rated by
his ability to anticipate his problems rather
than to meet them as they come.*
— HOWARD CONLEY

I had big plans for the morning as a substitute church school teacher for the class of two-year-old children. I had been thinking of my plan of action well in advance. I had studied the lesson plan, and I was prepared for an organized schedule of activities such as drawing with crayons, singing songs, and reading stories. I was confident this class session was going to be an educational, stimulating, and productive experience for every child.

My first clue that things might be a little more difficult than I imagined was when the fifth child arrived. Only after a few minutes of teaching the class and struggling with my wife to contain our little students, I experienced an epiphany. My wife and I were outnumbered. We only had four arms to contain their five little bodies.

About ten minutes into the ninety-minute session, even more little people had arrived and I abandoned any hope of being the proactive class leader that I had imagined just earlier that morning. I went quickly from being an educator to a disaster relief worker as I scurried around behind the tiny little human tornadoes, putting toys, crayons, blocks, trucks, and puzzles back in their respective places as fast as they could scatter them about the room.

Shortly before the class was to end, I was finding at least some consolation that we had survived the class without any serious incidents. Then I noticed a puddle on the floor. Apparently Sally gives a nonverbal signal when she needs to go the bathroom, and I had missed the signal.

As the last child left that morning, I was still picking small pieces of Play-doh molding clay from my hair and wondering what had just happened. An hour and a half earlier, I really did have a plan and some goals I wanted to accomplish. Now the class was over, and I wasn't exactly sure what I had accomplished other than delivering the toddlers all still living and breathing back to their parents.

For many people, Monday mornings are much like that toddler church school class. They start the week with high expectations and goals. Then they fall into a mode of managing chaos because they don't anticipate the many ordinary things that happen every Monday to disrupt their plans and distract them from their goals. Traffic tie-ups, social colleagues and employees, and work stations left unorganized from the previous Friday, quickly throw them out of the routine they planned. They end up running from one crisis to another until they find themselves lunging for the weekend so they can chance to catch their breath. This week, don't just prepare for the next Monday morning but anticipate and avoid the many ordinary things that can distract you from your focus. Getting organized for your week isn't enough. With our lives moving faster and becoming busier, the only way to achieve success and reach our goals is to anticipate problems and avoid them.

Many people start the week with high expectations and goals. Then they fall into a mode of managing chaos because they don't anticipate the many ordinary things that happen every Monday to disrupt their plans and distract them from their goals.

Write It Down

A man would do well to carry a pencil in his pocket, and write down the thoughts of the moment. Those that come unsought for are commonly the most valuable, and should be secured, because they seldom return.
— FRANCIS BACON

Van Gogh carried one with him. So did Henri Matisse and Ernest Hemingway. Not long ago, I purchased the same version of the little black notebook that many creative thinkers have used.

For years I had been jotting my ideas down on anything that I could get my hands on. I might have used a napkin, an event program, or a page torn out of a magazine to jot down an idea or thought that I didn't want to lose. But this was a problem, because these single little scraps of paper were susceptible to getting lost or thrown into the trash by my wife, who was unaware of their significance. Once the little piece of paper was lost, often my idea was lost as well, never to return to me again.

So now this little black book has become an important part of my life. I use it to record my thoughts, ideas, and dreams in one place so that I don't lose them. The notebook goes everywhere that I go because I never know when creative ideas might come to me. This kind of notebook was so important to creative thinkers like Van Gogh, Matisse, and Hemingway that on the inside cover of it they would offer a significant monetary reward for its return if lost and found.

What system do you have for recording your ideas and thoughts so that you don't forget them? Are you struggling to make your dreams come true, because you can't seem to remember to act upon your most creative and innovative ideas? Do the ideas you have far outnumber the ideas you make happen?

This week, implement a better system for recording your thoughts and ideas. Begin carrying a pen and notebook with you at all times in order to write down the thoughts of the moment. Avoid one of life's greatest tragedies, which is never acting upon, never pursuing, and never sharing life-changing and dream-fulfilling ideas. Those are the ideas that often come to us when we are not expecting them but then die a quick death because they are not written down and then are forgotten, never to return.

As I once heard a popular television commercial say, "It's not how many ideas you have but how many you make happen." You can only make your ideas happen if you record them at the moment they occur to you so that you will remember to act upon them later.

Begin carrying a pen and notebook with you at all times in order to write down the thoughts of the moment. Avoid one of life's greatest tragedies, which is never acting upon, never pursuing, and never sharing life-changing and dream-fulfilling ideas.

Speak Less and
Listen More

*Remember what Simonides said—that he
never repented that he had held his tongue,
but often that he had spoke.*

— PLUTARCH

I was watching racecar driver Jimmie Johnson not long ago as he accepted his award for finishing as one of the top racecar drivers on the NASCAR Winston Cup Circuit for 2002. Before a nationally televised audience in the United States, Johnson stepped to the microphone and proceeded to say "I'd like to thank a lot of awful people." He meant to thank "an awful lot of people." The audience responded with hearty laughter.

We have all had moments like Johnson had that night. When we are nervous, tired, or angry, our mouths don't always cooperate with our brains. We either don't speak the words right, or we don't speak the right words. Many times, the result we achieve with those words is worse than what Johnson experienced. Instead of laughter, our words cause hurt feelings and damage our reputation, credibility, and important relationships.

How many times have you spoken words only to later regret saying them? What damage have you caused to relationships with your friends, family, and colleagues because you didn't have the strength and wisdom to hold your tongue? Would you be more respected as a leader of your organization, team, or family if you spoke fewer words yourself and listened more to the words of others?

This week, remember that often the best thing you can do is hold your silence and be thoughtful when you speak. Resist the temptation to comment just for the sake of being heard when you really have nothing to add to a discussion. Think twice before you speak when you are nervous, tired, or angry. Speak less and listen more, and over time, you will be more admired and respected by those that you lead.

Would you be more respected as a leader
of your organization, team, or family if you
spoke fewer words yourself and listened
more to the words of others?

Know
the Time

It is later than you think.

— SUNDIAL INSCRIPTION

As the hotel shuttle van pulled away from the curb of the Greater Cincinnati Airport, the driver asked us, "How are you guys tonight?"

"Terrible, but thanks for asking," said Steve, the man sitting in front of me.

Steve had arrived at the airport from St. Louis, which follows the U.S. central time zone, earlier in the evening. Looking at his watch, set to central time, he thought he had plenty of time before boarding for his connecting flight to Jackson, Mississippi, so he sat down for a cup of coffee at Starbucks. Thirty minutes later, Steve told a man he had met there that his flight departed at 9 p.m. "You are going to miss your flight," said the man. It was only then that Steve realized that Cincinnati was on eastern time and not central time, and that it was 8:55 p.m. instead of 7:55 p.m.

"When I told the man that I had thought Cincinnati was on the central time zone and not the eastern time zone, he looked at me like I was the dumbest man in the world," said Steve. While relaxing at Starbucks, Steve had missed the last flight of the day to Jackson and had to spend the night in Cincinnati.

Time can get away from all of us, if we do not watch it carefully. Like Steve at the airport, we can be leisurely sipping coffee, relaxing and enjoying life, only to realize too late that important opportunities have passed us by. We move along through life, waiting to take action to pursue our dreams and thinking we know the time when actually it is often later than we think.

Do you know what time it is? Are you leisurely putting things off until tomorrow when it is really later than you think? What are the chances that you might have to admit one day that you let some important opportunity pass you by, because you did not realize it was time to act?

This week, begin taking the actions that will move you closer to achieving your dreams. Push yourself to do those things now that might be easier to put off until later. Commit yourself to doing things early rather than risking the possibility of being even a minute too late. Understand that even though you may think you know the time, it might be later than you think.

We move along through life, waiting to take action to pursue our dreams and thinking we know the time when actually it is often later than we think.

Make Time

You will never find time for anything. If you want time, you must make it.
— CHARLES BIXTON

I thought I found something the other day that was more valuable to me than money. I thought I found some time.

Although I enjoy *The Wall Street Journal,* I don't get to read it every day. The older I become, the less time I seem to have to read it. Not long ago, I noticed that the unread issues were beginning to stack up. I was looking for time to read them, but there didn't seem to be any.

Then one day while I was riding the exercise bicycle at the fitness center, it dawned on me. Why couldn't I read *The Wall Street Journal* while riding the stationary bicycle? I tried it and it worked. I thought at first I had found some time. But I didn't really find it, I had just decided to make more effective use of the

83

time I already had.

As we advance in age, we get a better appreciation of the value of time. I recall watching the clock as a young school boy thinking that time was passing so slowly! I thought each day would never end. Minutes seemed like hours. Now, as an adult, time passes so quickly that I cannot keep up with it. Hours seem like minutes. The worst thing about time as we grow older is that there never seems to be enough of it, and far too much of our time seems to be controlled by other people.

So, I have trained myself to make time for those things in life that are the most important. For instance, I have learned that I must steal at least fifteen minutes from each day to think creatively with nothing in front of me except a notepad. Sometimes I come up with ideas in those fifteen minutes that inspire these messages. Other times I think of new ways to be more effective in my personal and professional life. I have been surprised at how many creative ideas I can generate in such a short period of time.

The key to getting things done in life isn't finding the time to do them. If you are simply trying to find the time, you never will. You must make the time even if it means stealing it from another activity.

This week, make time each day for those things that are the most important but never seem to get done. Set aside at least fifteen minutes of the 1,440 minutes in each day to move yourself closer to achieving your long-term dreams.

The key to getting things done in life isn't finding the time to do them. You must make the time even if it means stealing it from another activity.

Keep Cool

Avoid letting temper block progress—
keep cool.
— WILLIAM FEATHER

"That's impossible," said the airline check-in counter attendant as I explained to him that I wanted to fly from my home city of Lexington to Atlanta, pick up my passport in Atlanta, and continue onward to Sao Paulo, Brazil. Due to time constraints, my passport and visa were being flown at the last minute from Washington to the airport in Atlanta. "The rules say that I cannot let you begin travel on an international ticket unless you have a passport at check-in," he said.

My stress level rose higher and higher as the departure time for the flight to Atlanta drew closer and the attendant's refusal to give me a boarding pass for the flight grew stronger. There was only one flight per day from Atlanta to Sao Paulo, and missing this flight to Atlanta would jeopardize the entire trip.

After a few minutes of conversation, the attendant was ready to assist the next passenger in the queue. "Mr. Rector," he said, "there's simply nothing I can do for you unless you have your passport."

Calmly and coolly, I started to turn away from the counter but then I had an idea. "I know this is an unusual situation I've presented to you and I thank you for the time you've spent with me, but would you mind at least calling the international desk of the airline to see if they might have an idea on how to get me to Atlanta on this ticket without a passport."

The attendant looked at the people behind me in the line, hesitated, but then picked up the telephone and called the international desk of the airline. Within a couple of minutes, the person at the international desk had explained to him how he could put me on the flight to Atlanta and he was soon printing out my boarding pass.

Over the years, there have been times when I have faced such stressful situations and lost my temper when I wasn't getting what I wanted or expected from a business. But, having kept my cool that day, I was much more likely to get what I wanted. Had I made the attendant angry, I doubt that he would have taken the time to call the international desk in light of the many people waiting in line behind me.

Successful leaders know that losing their tempers blocks their progress more than helps their cause. They understand that they are more likely to get their complaint addressed, get a refund, or get any desired remedy as customers if they maintain a pleasant conversation with the representative of the business. They know that when they lose their tempers, raise their voices, demand, or even threaten people, they are less likely to achieve the results they desire.

Do you keep your cool as a customer in even the most stressful situations? Are you able to maintain your composure even when the representative of the business is acting in an unreasonable or outrageous way? Does losing your temper often cause others to become defensive and make it less likely for you to achieve the results you desire?

This week, remember to keep your cool when faced with difficult situations, not only as a customer, but also as a leader of your organization, team, or family. Don't let your temper block your progress. Keep cool in all situations. It will help you achieve your goals and even make the impossible become possible.

*Successful leaders know that losing their
tempers blocks their progress
more than helps their cause.*

Do What
You Can

While we are postponing, life speeds by.
— SENECA

As I looked out the window of my room in the Sheraton Hotel in Lagos, Nigeria, I could see heavy rain falling on the complex jogging track below me. With the hotel fitness center closed because of damage caused by a recent storm, I was tempted to forget about the exercise workout I had planned. The only place to exercise seemed to be my hotel room.

I resisted the urge, strong as it was, to work or to take a nap. I moved the furniture around and strapped on my CD player and earphones. To the beat of the music, I began jogging back and forth, twelve steps at a time, across the room. I added in a few jumping jacks and push-ups from time to time. After thirty minutes, my heart was pounding, and I had worked up a good sweat.

After the workout, I felt much better physically and much less tired from jet lag, than I did prior to the workout. But an even more important benefit to me was a great sense of accomplishment. It would have been so easy for me to have used the circumstances as a good excuse to skip exercising that day. In fact, that is what I've done more often than not so many times before while traveling.

I want to become better at overcoming excuses in more aspects of my life than just my exercise while traveling, because I know that people who make a great impact upon the lives of others are disciplined enough to be productive no matter what the circumstances. They do not wait for perfect conditions before they take action. They do what they can, wherever they are, with what they have.

For example, young Anne Frank kept a diary while hiding with her family for two years in a canal-side house in Amsterdam. Although she later died in a Nazi concentration camp in 1945, her diary has been translated into more than sixty languages and her words have inspired millions over the years, including Nelson Mandela, who said in 1994 that he "derived much encouragement from it" during his long confinement in a South African prison.

Are you giving a full effort to those tasks that are important to you or are you waiting for better circumstances? Do you control excuses or do excuses control you? Is life speeding by you while you are postponing action until the conditions are perfect?

This week, understand that the conditions for you to take action will probably never be perfect. Drink from the cup of life and make a productive use of every moment whether it's moving yourself toward achieving your dreams, strengthening your spirituality, or connecting with your loved ones. Do what you can, wherever you are, with what you have, every day.

People who make a great impact upon the lives of others are disciplined enough to be productive no matter what the circumstances. They do not wait for perfect conditions before they take action. They do what they can, wherever they are, with what they have.

Make the Best of It

*The lure of the distant and the difficult is
deceptive. The great opportunity is
where you are.*
— John Burroughs

*A pessimist is one who makes difficulties of
his opportunities; an optimist is one who
makes opportunities of his difficulties.*
— Reginald B. Mansell

Our car had come to a stop on a four-lane high-
way in Lagos, Nigeria. There was a long line of cars ahead of us,
all sitting bumper to bumper. The driver of our car said to us,
"We are not going to be moving any time soon." Such is a typical
occurrence in this city of 12 million people, which has some of

the worst traffic congestion in the world.

While we sat in the traffic jam, several people approached the car to try to sell us various products. They were selling everything you can imagine: snacks, shoes, clothes, electrical appliances, newspapers, etc. I joked to my friends that it was the first "highway shopping mall" I had ever seen.

What impressed me the most about this experience was how the Nigerian people respond to this frustrating situation. As they do with many great challenges, annoyances, and inconveniences that face this city, they simply choose to make the best of it, no matter what difficulty is presented to them. The people selling the products in the streets see more than just a huge traffic jam; they view it as a large captive audience and marketplace to pursue their entrepreneurial dreams.

And instead of letting the salespeople add to their irritation, the drivers take advantage of the situation to buy what they need. In fact, sales of products in the streets during traffic jams is so successful in Lagos that many companies choose to launch new products there rather than in stores.

Making the best of difficult situations is an important ability that all great leaders develop. They don't wait for better times to come their way. They realize that the greatest opportunities are often where they are now, rather than way off in the distance. They learn to be adaptable and flexible and to make the best of whatever may come their way.

How do you deal with frustrating situations? Do you respond to difficult circumstances by giving up and waiting for a better day, even though you do not know if that better day will ever come? Do you sit still complaining about not being able to reach your intended destination fast enough instead of looking around you for the great opportunities that may exist where you are now?

This week, look for opportunity even in the most annoying and challenging situations. Do not become so focused upon your long-term dreams that you ignore great short-term opportunities along the way. Learn to see opportunities even in your difficulties, and make the best of whatever situation you find yourself in every day.

Making the best of difficult situations is an important ability that all great leaders develop. They don't wait for better times to come their way. They realize that the greatest opportunities are often where they are now, rather than way off in the distance.

Add Variety

Undertake to do something that is difficult; it will do you good. Unless you try to do something beyond what you have already mastered, you will never grow.
— RONALD E. OSBORN

For two years now, my main form of daily exercise has been running on a treadmill. But with the New Year beginning, I decided that maybe it was time to push myself out of my comfort zone and try something different. Over the past few months, several people had suggested that I try a stationary bicycling class to add a little variety to my exercise routine. I finally decided to try it.

After mounting my bike, one of twenty in the dark classroom, I asked the woman seated on the bike next to me, "When are they going to turn on the lights?"

"We like it dark in here," she said. "It helps us to imagine that we are really going up and down hills even though our bikes are stationary." About twelve minutes into the class and gasping for air, I realized that the real reason they keep it dark is so that you won't be discouraged by the sight of the many people who have collapsed onto the floor from exhaustion during the class. My leg muscles were getting tighter and hurting more with each turn of the foot pedals.

Well into the session, the instructor came over to my bike. She asked me for my name. When I told her my name, she said, "Bruce! That'll be easy to remember; my brother's name is Bruce." I thought how nice it was of her to come over during the class simply to be friendly and to learn my name. So I was surprised when seconds later, she was back on her bicycle at the front of the class and shouting to the whole class through her microphone, "Come on, Bruce, pedal faster, pick up the pace!" Later I was told that she had given birth to her third child only a month or so earlier. After the doctor cut the umbilical cord of her newborn child, she allegedly jumped off the bed, wiped the sweat from her forehead, and began doing push-ups and sit-ups.

When the class was over, I crawled up the stairs to the locker room and went on with my day. I was so tired that I thought I would have no energy to exercise for the next several days. But the following day, I actually felt pretty good, and running on the treadmill was much easier for me than it had been before the bicycle class. I learned that by pushing myself to experience a different physical activity, I was making myself stronger in my main area of exercise: a principle of physical conditioning called "cross-training."

Successful people know the importance of "cross-training" with regard to their mental, spiritual, and physical conditioning. They frequent the company of a diverse group of people who are smarter, more disciplined, and more experienced than themselves. They read a wide variety of books that will challenge them to think of new approaches to innovate and become better. They seek experiences that take them out of their comfort zones and cause them to build broader bases of skills that will make them even stronger in their core endeavors.

What are you doing to cross-train yourself? When was the last time you undertook to do something new and difficult? What skills are you trying to develop beyond the ones you have already mastered?

This week, think about how you can put more variety into your life. Frequent the company of those people you most admire for having the discipline and wisdom you would like to have. Grow stronger as a person and as a leader by pushing yourself to master new skills and talents beyond the ones you have already mastered.

Successful people know the importance of "cross-training" with regard to their mental, spiritual, and physical conditioning. They seek experiences that take them out of their comfort zones and cause them to build broader bases of skills that will make them even stronger in their core endeavors.

Live Out Loud

*Wake the neighbors. Get the word out. Crank
up the music, climb a mountain, and shout.
This is life we've been given, made
to be lived out. So, live out loud.*
— STEVEN CURTIS CHAPMAN

At 5:30 in the morning, I'm on the exercise
treadmill. About 2.5 kilometers (1.5 miles) into the run, I am
hitting full stride. A pulsating beat of great music is playing through
my headphones. I feel as if I could run forever.

Later in the morning, I'm driving my car to my office. It's one
of those fantastic Kentucky sunrises that make living here so special. The temperature is cool and crisp. The sun is rising over the
rolling hills. Without a single cloud, the sky is so clear and such
a shade of light blue that I can see the moon through my open
sunroof as well as the rising sun through my windshield.

Everything has come together so well this morning, I feel nothing can stop me. I believe I can fly. I believe I can touch the sky. I feel great, and I want the world to know it. I will perform better in everything that I do this day because I am ready to live out loud.

Wouldn't you like to start every day ready to live out loud? How much more fulfilling would our lives be if we began each day so pumped about those things that we are the most passionate about (our faith, our family, our work) that we wanted to share our excitement with others? How much greater an impact would we have on the people around us if the way we walked and carried ourselves conveyed to them that we were confident that this was going to be a great day?

This week, think of what might help you to get off to a great start each day. You might not be able to control the weather, but you can control your morning routine. Begin choosing activities, a diet, and music that will put you in the frame of mind you need to have a great day. Prepare yourself to take advantage of each new day you've been given and to live out loud.

How much greater an impact would we have on the people around us if the way we walked and carried ourselves conveyed to them that we were confident that this was going to be a great day?

Begin Paddling

The life of every man is a diary in which he means to write one story, and writes another, and his humblest hour is when he compares the volume as it is with what he vowed to make it.

— JAMES M. BARRIE

There were faster, more stylish, and more complicated boats, but the boat that my father loved the most was the canoe. I have fond memories of the many canoe trips that I enjoyed with my father.

With a canoe, the type of water you are navigating makes a big difference in determining the amount of effort that you need to expend with your paddle in order to get where you want to go. Most of the time, we paddled our way across lakes, where changing direction and getting to where you wanted to go was fairly easy. But sometimes we traveled down a river, creek, or stream, and controlling our direction was much more difficult.

The current of a river changes canoeing. A strong current allows you to drift along without paddling, but it can also take you in a different direction than you want to go unless you pay constant attention to where you are headed. And I recall one occasion where my father intended to stop at a particular city along the river, but the current was so swift that it carried him well past his intended destination. The result was that he had to take out the canoe far downstream from where my mother was to pick us up, and then humbly make a telephone call to have her drive the car to meet us at our new destination.

Millions of people around the world reach the twilight years of their lives having never chased their own personal dreams because they were too busy working for someone else to take the time to do what they really wanted to do. They are gliding down the river of life, letting the current take them in a direction they do not want to go.

In the river of life, we are each given our own canoe and a paddle. Some people know where they want to go with their canoe, but never put the oar in the water, content to travel wherever the flow of the river takes them. Others paddle a little, drift a little, paddle a little, drift a little, and on and on, sometimes reaching their intended destination, but too many times only filled with regret at the end of the journey.

The river of life is changing today. The current is getting stronger and faster because of technology and the dynamics of the new economy. The once calm river streams are now fast moving rapids, and once we start to drift with the current, it can become almost impossible to turn the canoe around. With even the slightest bit of inattention, we have drifted way downstream before we realize it.

Where do you want to go with your canoe in the river of life? You probably know. You probably have your own dreams. Maybe you want to start your own business? Maybe you want to enter a different career? Maybe you want to develop a music talent or hobby? Maybe you merely want to travel and appreciate the beauty and diversity of the world?

Whatever your goal, just remember that the river of life is moving along, and the longer you wait, the more likely you will be to be looking back on your life, thankful for the wonderful things you accomplished, but regretting having never chased your dreams. This week, put your oar in the water and begin moving your canoe in the direction you want it to go, before you must humbly admit that it's too late.

Millions of people around the world reach the twilight years of their lives having never chased their own personal dreams because they were too busy working for someone else to take the time to do what they really wanted to do. They are gliding down the river of life, letting the current take them in a direction they do not want to go. Where do you want to go with your canoe in the river of life?

Use Your
Resources

*Small opportunities are often the beginning
of great enterprises.*
— DEMOSTHENES

As we walked around the garden in Fukui, Japan, my friend Keita pointed out to me the many aspects of Japanese architecture that maximize the use of natural resources. He told me that the house at the edge of the pond had been designed so that the reflection of sunlight on the water would illuminate the rooms inside it. Keita pointed out other places in the building and the surrounding garden where the architect had used the effects of wind, light, water, and air. He said that an important principle of Japanese architecture is to take advantage of every opportunity to use a natural resource.

Like traditional Japanese architects, great leaders also make use of all the resources they are given. They understand their strengths and talents. They recognize and respect small as well as big opportunities. They work diligently to make sure no resource is wasted, even if it means giving it away to someone else who might make better use of it.

Is your daily life an example of efficiency and maximum use of resources? Are you fully using your talents and gifts to prepare yourself to meet opportunity when it comes your way? Do you often ignore, dismiss, or waste small opportunities that could lead to great things for you or for someone else?

This week, spend a few moments listing all the talents, gifts, and opportunities, no matter how small, with which you have been blessed. Then modify your daily routine if necessary to maximize your use of them. Make today the day you begin making use of all you have been given and prepare yourself to meet the opportunities that will enable you to achieve your dreams.

Are you fully using your talents and gifts to prepare yourself to meet opportunity when it comes your way? Do you often ignore, dismiss, or waste small opportunities that could lead to great things for you or for someone else?

III. Social Awareness

Be Accessible to Advice

*Do not be inaccessible. None is so perfect
that he does not need at times
the advice of others.*
— BALTASAR GRACIAN

*No man is so foolish but he may sometimes
give another good counsel, and no man so
wise that he might easily err if he takes no
other counsel than his own. He that is taught
only by himself has a fool for a master.*
— BEN JOHNSON

As I was exercising at the athletic club, I came
up with an idea that I thought would make my workouts and
those of the other members more enjoyable. I walked over to a

club staff member and made my suggestion to him.

The young staff member gave me a response that I really wasn't expecting. "I'm not authorized to take suggestions. If you'd like to make a suggestion, you'll have to talk to my supervisor," he said, pointing to a man across the room.

I walked over to the supervisor, and he told me that he wasn't authorized to take suggestions either. He said the only way to make a suggestion about the athletic club was to write it down and then place it in the suggestion box. I began looking around the room for a hidden camera, figuring that this had to be one of those crazy television shows like *Candid Camera*. But, there was no camera. He was serious. I thanked him for his time and began my search for the suggestion box.

In my many prior visits to the athletic club, I had not noticed a suggestion box. Now realizing the great importance of the box in the customer service and quality improvement strategy of the club, I was sure that I had just overlooked it.

I searched around the athletic club for the suggestion box that day but didn't see one and finally just gave up on sharing my idea. Then several weeks later, while getting a drink at one of the water fountains at the club, I saw a waist-high stand with a small box at the top. There was no sign on or around it indicating its purpose. There was an ink pen chained to the top of the box, but no paper. Another member was standing nearby, and I asked him what the box was for, and he said, "I think it's a suggestion box." You might think that the athletic club's method of handling suggestions sounds outrageous, but many people handle receiving advice and counsel from others the same way. They say they welcome suggestions as to how they might improve themselves, but at the same time they try very hard to make themselves inaccessible to them.

No person is so perfect that he or she could not benefit from suggestions, but yet we often respond to them with reluctance, defensiveness, and anger. We resist advice even though the counsel that we might receive from those around us, our family, customers, and colleagues, is often more valuable and more pure than the perspective we get from our own understanding which is saturated by personal biases, customs, and traditions.

How accessible are you to advice? Do you solicit suggestions in a way that makes people really believe that you welcome and appreciate frank and honest feedback? Do you respond to advice with a thankful and appreciative attitude or with defensiveness and poor listening?

Make an effort this week to show others that you want and appreciate their advice. Invite others to give suggestions to you in a way that will inspire them to do so. Realize that people will only share good ideas with you if they believe you are accessible to them. Create an environment around you, your team, and your organization that shows you value and welcome good counsel and honest advice.

We resist advice even though the counsel that we might receive from those around us is often more valuable and more pure than the perspective we get from our own understanding which is saturated by personal biases, customs, and traditions.

Maintain Simple Surroundings

I am not drowning in a sea of opportunity,
but I am swimming very hard.
— Frances Hesselbein

The sun was rising as I jogged through the streets of the beautiful city of Levadia. Surrounded by mountains, this region of Greece is full of ancient history. Thousands of years ago, nearby Delphi was once considered the center of the world.

During my exercise run that morning, I passed a series of fantastic waterfalls that originate at the foot of the mountains and then wind through the heart of Levadia. As I jogged along the river's edge out of the city and into the mountains, I noticed how simple my surroundings had become. There were only a few trees and shrubs covering the rocks and dirt on the mountainsides. The only sound I could hear other than my own footsteps was the sound of the wind blowing through the rocks. I was so impressed with the scenery, that I stopped to rest and to enjoy the moment.

As I sat on a rock, on the hillside, I took note of the simplicity of my surroundings. I thought about the many Greek philosophers who once roamed these same hills and mountains to think, exchange information, and share ideas. I wondered how much this uncomplicated environment might have enabled them to express the many thoughts and ideas that were inscribed upon the walls of nearby ruins and that are still used today, such as "Know Thyself" and "Everything in Moderation."

Business, government, and family leaders today often find their lives more hectic and complicated than ever. Technology and success create opportunity, which in turn creates more success and even more opportunity. At some point, opportunities become so overwhelming that our ability to think clearly and to be productive declines.

Great leaders understand the importance of managing the technology, success, and opportunity that surrounds them. They know that to accomplish significant goals they must be able to think clearly. They work hard to keep their surroundings simple. They do not hesitate to say "no" to even wonderful opportunities when accepting them would make their lives too complicated. They realize that technology can actually make them less productive rather than more productive. They resist the temptation to let success pull them away from maintaining the very habits that made them successful.

How are you dealing with your sea of opportunity? Has your life become so dominated by technology, success, and opportunity that you now have trouble thinking clearly? Simplify your life this week so that you can think, share information, and exchange ideas more clearly, and make a lasting impact upon the world.

Great leaders understand the importance of managing the technology, success, and opportunity that surrounds them. They know that to accomplish significant goals they must be able to think clearly. They work hard to keep their surroundings simple.

Let Them
Do It

*You cannot help men permanently
by doing for them what they could and
should do for themselves.*
— ABRAHAM LINCOLN

"No, Dad; let me do it." Those are words that I am beginning to hear more often from my son as he ventures through his fourth year of life. As he grows taller and stronger, he is also becoming more independent.

Although my wife and I find ourselves having less to do to physically care for him, in many ways, his increasing ability to do things for himself is making our parenting more difficult. When he was first born, we had to do everything for him. But now we must separate those things we should do for him from those he can and should do for himself.

Family leaders aren't the only ones who face this difficult choice of deciding how much to do for others. Business, community, and government leaders face the same dilemma. The more successful we become and the more our team grows, the harder it becomes to do everything ourselves. The hands-on and "I'll-just-do-it-myself" mentality limits the potential of the organization and eventually can lead to the physical and mental exhaustion of the leader.

Still, leaders often focus too much on the short-term benefits of getting the work done faster and better by doing it themselves. They resist the need to improve their delegation, mentoring, and teaching skills needed to empower employees and team members and to help the organization become more successful in the long run.

Are you doing too much for the individuals you supervise and lead? Are you delegating your work with enough clarity and details, or are your instructions too ambiguous and vague? Do you invest enough time in training and teaching those around you so that they may become more independent and help the organization become more successful in the long run?

Ask yourself this week how much more you and your organization could accomplish through empowering every team member to become more independent. Analyze the way you delegate, review, and improve the work of those you lead. And remember that the worst thing you can do for others (as well as for yourself and your organization) is doing something they could and should be doing for themselves.

The more successful we become and the more our team grows, the harder it becomes to do everything ourselves. The hands-on and "I'll-just-do-it-myself" mentality limits the potential of the organization and eventually can lead to the physical and mental exhaustion of the leader.

Hang On

Success seems to be largely a matter of
hanging on after others have let go.
— WILLIAM FEATHER

After a long day at work, I finally reach the couch at my home. I settle in and close my eyes, hoping to rest my mind and body and feeling as if I have given all the effort I can for one day.

Only seconds after I begin to relax, a small hand grabs mine and the young child at the other end of it asks me to put in a little more activity before I end my day. "Up, Daddy," my son pleads. "Outside, Daddy," he directs me after I have risen to my feet. "March, Daddy!" And off we go around the yard singing "M-I-C-K-E-Y M-O-U-S-E" to the tune of the famous Disney song.

Each evening, my son gives me the little push that I need to make the last several hours of my day the best ones. Although my mind and body tell me I have given all I can, my son encourages me to "hang on" a little longer.

We all need someone like my son in our lives to help us to hang on at times when we feel like giving up. We need people around us who will hold us accountable for finishing what we started. We need friends and loyal teammates who care enough to push us to continue when others would just sit back and watch us quit. The people who push us to hang on after others have let go are the ones that do the most to help us become successful.

This week, think about the people around you that will help you press on when you feel like quitting. Surround yourself with friends and colleagues who will hold you accountable and push you to give an extra effort. To be successful, you must hang on when others are letting go, and there are times when all of us need a push or pull, even if it comes from the very small hand of a child, to do what we must.

The people who push us to hang on after others have let go are the ones that do the most to help us become successful.

Truly
Understand

*Three-fourths of the mistakes a man makes
are made because he does not really know the
things he thinks he knows.*
— JAMES BRYCE

It was my first visit to Scotland, and even though
I was in a foreign country, I expected things to be going a little
more smoothly. Here I was at the Glasgow train station trying to
order my meal at a familiar American restaurant chain, Burger
King, and I was having little success in getting the young lady
across the counter to understand my order. We were both speak-
ing English, but her Scottish accent and my Midwestern American accent made our conversation difficult. I finally just took
whatever she had put into my bag, smiled at her, and went on my
way.

You may not have had exactly the same experience as mine at that Burger King in Scotland, but you have probably experienced a similarly troublesome communication failure. The communication failure that takes place when we think we understand the other person, but we actually don't.

There are a number of ways in which we might find ourselves thinking that we understand people when we actually don't. As a team leader, we think we know what motivates our team members to perform at their highest levels although we can't recall the last time we asked them. We think our business partners have the same vision for the enterprise we do, but we've never confirmed it by putting a mission and vision statement into writing. We think we are attuned to the needs of our spouses and children, but we find our lives to be so busy that we seem to pass each other in our homes every day with little more than smiles and superficial conversations.

This week, fight the natural tendency to assume things that you don't really know. Ask yourself whether you really know what those you work with and live with are thinking. Take a little extra time to make sure you truly understand what's going on in the lives of the people around you and how you can help each other to improve and grow stronger. Avoid making some of the mistakes that you might be inclined to make by thinking that you know more about them than you really know.

Ask yourself whether you really know what
those you work with and live with are thinking.

Improve Your Reputation

To disregard what the world thinks of us is
not only arrogant but utterly shameless.
— CICERO

The way to gain a good reputation is to
endeavor to be what you desire to appear.
— SOCRATES

Eating toast and drinking coffee at the kitchen table at my friend James' home in Dublin, Ireland, I noticed a small sign James had posted on his refrigerator. The sign said: "Accountants are boring and mean."

"A friend posted it there some time ago as a joke," said James. "I decided to keep it there because each morning I wanted to see it as I eat my breakfast and remind myself how the world perceives my profession." James explained that focusing on this perception as he begins each day helps him try harder during the day to prove it wrong.

Unlike James, many people never improve their reputations and images because they refuse to acknowledge how people around them might perceive them. And even if they do regularly ask for and receive feedback describing their weaknesses, they often do nothing in response to overcome them.

Outstanding leaders care about how others perceive them because it helps them see blind spots. They are not only open to criticism and suggestions from others, they are also able to draw conclusions from that feedback and then define concrete steps for improvement. They identify their perceived weaknesses and then endeavor to improve each day.

Is your image of yourself different from the image others have of you? What do the people closest to you perceive to be your weaknesses? How could you remind yourself, as you begin each day, of what you need to improve?

This week, gather input as to how others perceive you, then acknowledge your weaknesses and endeavor each day to be the person you aspire to be. Find creative ways to remind yourself of your need to change the perceptions of those around you. Get the most out of life by refusing to accept your shortcomings. Focus on gaining a better reputation and, in the process, improve yourself and help those around you.

Outstanding leaders care about how others perceive them because it helps them see blind spots. They identify their perceived weaknesses and then endeavor to improve each day.

Enter With
Eyes Open

Only those who can get into scrapes with
their eyes open can find a safe way out.
— LOGAN PEARSALL SMITH

The other day, I went to the store to purchase a new pair of blue jeans. Finding a pair the same size I purchased a year before, I took them to the dressing room to try them on.

They were a little tight, but I kept trying to pull them up. Thinking that they should fit me because I hadn't gained any weight, I continued to pull harder and harder, determined to get them on.

I struggled so hard that I lost my balance and fell hard against the door, hitting my elbow and letting go a loud yell of pain. "Something's going on in there; we'd better call for help," someone said from outside the booth. I yelled that I was okay, but no one seemed to hear me. "Assistance needed in men's clothing, code four," I heard over the loudspeaker. Panicking, I struggled frantically to pull the jeans off, and then I fell again. This time I scraped my head against the door latch. Now I was not only in pain, but my forehead was bleeding.

Eventually, I escaped from the jeans and the dressing booth. On my way out, I felt curious eyes on me. Someone offered me a tissue to wipe the blood off my forehead, but I was too humiliated to accept it.

My trip to buy a pair of blue jeans that day reminded me of a couple of important facts of life. First, as we get older, although our weight may not change, the shape of our body may, and we have to humbly go up in size every once in a while. And secondly, every time we enter a situation, we should not be so focused on getting in that we forget to prepare to gracefully get out when required.

Great leaders always have an exit plan, even when they are dedicated to a task. They understand that every great opportunity has at least some risk and an exit plan is always needed. They stay on guard, even while plans appear to be on course. They expect the unexpected and are ready to leave quickly if needed.

What is your exit plan for those projects you are currently working on with all your energy? Are you as ready for the unexpected as you are for the expected? Are you as prepared to get out of the project or endeavor as you were to get in?

This week, focus on going into new situations with your eyes open. Be aware of your surroundings and acknowledge that things might not go as planned. Maintain your guard and prepare for the unexpected, even if everything appears to be going well. Go in with your eyes open so that, if needed, you can safely walk out.

Great leaders always have an exit plan, even when they are dedicated to a task. They understand that every great opportunity has at least some risk and an exit plan is always needed. They stay on guard, even while plans appear to be on course. They expect the unexpected and are ready to leave quickly if needed.

Give Others
the Credit

I live by these three rules:
If anything goes bad, I did it.
If anything goes semi-good, we did it.
If anything goes real good, you did it.
— PAUL "BEAR" BRYANT

While visiting Oslo, Norway, as part of a large group tour, we stopped at a hotel for lunch. There were about thirty of us seated at a long table with five large candles spaced along the table. I sat at the end of the table with my wife and my three-year-old son Trevor.

Across the table from us was Mariona, who was playing throughout the lunch with Trevor. Toward the end of the lunch, Trevor was unsuccessfully trying to blow out the candle that was directly in front of him. Mariona asked Trevor to blow one more time. As he did, Mariona put her hand in front of her own mouth so Trevor could not see her and blew out the candle. Trevor looked surprised as several around him applauded and gave him all the praise for the accomplishment.

Trevor was soon focused on the next candle on the table and then on the next and on the next. As he blew air from his mouth, those sitting close to his target candle hid their mouths and blew. Out went the flame each time and there was applause for Trevor. This continued until Trevor reared back to blow out the fifth and final candle, at the opposite end of the table, fifteen meters away. Again, someone near the candle blew it out. This time the entire table erupted in applause for Trevor, causing him to feel like he had done it all by himself again.

Just as my friends were willing to give the praise for their own efforts to Trevor to make him feel good about himself, outstanding leaders don't mind doing important work to affect the outcome while giving others on the team the credit for a good result. They accept responsibility when things go poorly, but praise others when things go well. They are willing to humbly let others have the spotlight, even when it is their own effort that was the main cause of the success.

How do you handle the disappointments and successes of the team you lead? Are you quick to defend your own actions and to blame others when the results are less than you desired? Do you accept praise for successes too selfishly, or do you offer those supporting you, even in minor roles, the chance to share in it?

Examine your leadership style this week to make sure you are accepting responsibility for disappointments and motivating your team by sharing the praise with others. Begin giving others the credit even when your own efforts may have had a greater impact on the result. Turn the spotlight from the leader of any successful enterprise and begin focusing it more on those around you.

Outstanding leaders don't mind doing important work to affect the outcome while giving others on the team the credit for a good result. They accept responsibility when things go poorly, but praise others when things go well. They are willing to humbly let others have the spotlight, even when it is their own effort that was the main cause of the success.

Forgive and
Be Forgiven

Forgive many things in others;
nothing in yourself.

— AUSONIUS

They who forgive most,
shall be most forgiven.

— JOSIAH W. BAILEY

Built as a military fortification against intrusion, parts of the famous Great Wall of China were first constructed in 770 B.C. It is a massive structure said to be visible from the moon. It is a solid structure that throughout the centuries has proven to be impenetrable by outside forces. I was excited about my first chance to see and climb it.

With each step I took up the stairs of the Great Wall, my heart pounded faster and faster. The steps were very steep, and I had to pause several times to catch my breath. After passing several beacon towers where guards once watched for potential invaders, I stopped to rest.

Leaning over the edge, I viewed the magnificence of the wall ahead of me and behind me. As I looked down, I thought about some walls I've built in my own life. Not walls made of stones, but communication walls that I've built between others and myself when they have disappointed or angered me. I wondered if the "great walls" I have built were just as impenetrable, not only keeping out the bad, but also keeping out the good.

Great leaders are careful not to build such "great walls." They readily forgive others for mistakes they would never make themselves. Events may cause them to lose trust and respect for a person, but they never shut that person totally out. They understand the importance of keeping their friends close but their enemies closer. They also realize that for their own mistakes to be forgiven, they must be willing to forgive the mistakes of others.

What "great walls" have you built during your life? Are you keeping someone away from you because of a past mistake he or she has made that should have been long ago forgiven and forgotten? Are grudges you are keeping against others and your unwillingness to communicate with others denying you the opportunity to grow, learn, and live a more fulfilling life?

This week reflect upon your own life and identify great walls that you have built. Work harder in the future to forgive many things in others even though you expect better from yourself. Resist the temptation to build a great wall around yourself when you become angry and avoid suffering more from your anger than you do from the very thing that made you angry in the first place.

Great leaders are careful not to build "great walls." They readily forgive others for mistakes they would never make themselves. They understand the importance of keeping their friends close but their enemies closer. They also realize that for their own mistakes to be forgiven, they must be willing to forgive the mistakes of others.

Seek
Encouragement

*One of the most important but one of the
most difficult things for a powerful mind is to
be its own master.*
— JOSEPH ADDISON

In late 1999 and early 2000, I learned a great
deal about babies, mothers, and pregnancy. All fascinating stuff
for a guy whose only experience in the delivery room was in the
role of baby in 1963. Apparently a lot has changed about the
birthing process since that time.

In many societies today, fathers are not only expected to be
present in the delivery room, but they also take an active role in
the process. In America, it is common for the father to be given
the title of "Birthing Coach." I wondered at first exactly what a
birthing coach did, but after taking a class on the subject, I have

learned that the role of the birthing coach is to keep the mother focused on the goal of delivering the baby and to keep her mind off the pain that accompanies labor. The teacher at our birthing class described two ways that the father (birthing coach) accomplishes this:

1   If the baby exits the birth canal normally, with its face toward the mother's spine, the father's job is pretty easy. The father helps the mother concentrate on her breathing patterns. This keeps her mind off the painful contractions that come and go throughout the many hours of labor. During the breaks between painful contractions, the father feeds the mother ice chips; updates her on the latest football, basketball, and hockey scores; accepts her apologies for all the mean things she said about him during the prior contraction; and generally reassures her that everything is going well.

2   If the baby exits the birth canal with its head facing away from the mother's spine, the father has a much tougher job. This is called "back labor." The back of the baby's head presses against the mother's spine, and there are no breaks in the pain at all during the many hours of labor. The teacher said that in this kind of labor, the mother spends most of the time standing tall in the stirrups with her hands wrapped tightly around the father's neck. The father struggles to pry the mother's fingers off his neck long enough to get an occasional breath. This explains why some of the biggest and toughest fathers are seen crying or even passing out in the delivery room.

We all know that having a coach in the delivery room isn't absolutely necessary. Throughout history many women have given birth to children without a coach. But today, even though a mother could get by without it, in many cultures having a birthing coach is generally accepted as a smart thing to do.

Likewise, lots of us go throughout our business and personal lives without coaches, and many of us do just fine. But, perhaps, if having a personal coach can work so effectively in other processes such as childbirth, doesn't it make sense to have a coach in those areas of our lives as well?

What painful process do you have to endure to reach your goals? Would you make more progress in reaching your goals if you had a "coach" to hold you accountable and keep you focused? If having a coach makes people better athletes, actors, and dancers, could having a coach make you a better leader, business owner, or parent?

Controlling our own minds is more than just utilizing the power of positive thinking. It involves maintaining concentration, exercising commitment, and avoiding temptation. There is no better vehicle for pursuing your dreams than a powerful mind, but sometimes our minds need a little outside encouragement in order to help us to reach our potential. This week, ask yourself whether or not you might become a better leader, person, and parent if you had someone coaching you and holding you accountable.

What painful process do you have to endure to reach your goals? Would you make more progress in reaching your goals if you had a "coach" to hold you accountable and keep you focused?

Look Deeper

A soul that sees beauty may sometimes walk alone.
— JOHANN WOLFGANG VON GOETHE

Those who skim over the surface in a hit-or-miss fashion not only forfeit the best returns on their efforts, but are ever barred from the pleasure of seeing beauty in the results of their labor.
— RODERICK STEVENS

The sun was shining brightly as Andre and I drove across the beautiful Swiss countryside on our way from Geneva to Bern. The temperature was a fair 50 degrees Fahrenheit (10 degrees Celsius). It was such a nice day that we soon found ourselves caught up in the moment and singing along with Aretha Franklin, oblivious to how the drivers of other cars might perceive us, as she belted out "R-E-S-P-E-C-T" through the car stereo speakers.

As nice as it was that day and as much fun as Andre and I were having, there was one thing missing. A low level of thin clouds and fog prevented us from seeing the beautiful Swiss Alps that would have normally been visible on the horizon. "What a pity," said Andre, "that you are here on such a fantastic day, but you cannot see the Alps."

After Andre's comment, I was determined to look deeper through the clouds until I could see the Alps. Throughout the rest of the day I was stretching and twisting my neck trying to get a glimpse of them everywhere I went. But it wasn't until the very last few minutes of daylight that it finally happened.

Standing on the Kirchenfeld Bridge in the city of Bern as the day concluded, the rays of the setting sun broke through the low clouds and finally illuminated the Alps in the distance with a brilliant red glow which was one of the most spectacular scenes I have ever witnessed. The Swiss Alps had been there all along even though I could not see them. It was only by persisting to look deeper, that I achieved such a breathtaking view.

Today our lives are busier than ever largely because the technology has increased the amount of information that we are asked to process each day. As a result, our relationships and the way we do our work can easily become more and more superficial. Too often we are moving around and processing information so quickly, that we don't take enough time to look deeper to reveal the true beauty of the people we are meeting and the work we are doing.

Are you happily singing along as you travel the road of life without taking the time to look for the true and deeper meaning of it? Do you maintain superficial relationships with people you love and work with rather than taking the time to discover the inner beauty that really drives and motivates them? Is there a far more spectacular and breathtaking view of the world right there for you to see if you will only take the time to look deeper and find it?

This week, devote more time and effort to understanding more deeply the people and projects that are an important part of life. Take some time to appreciate more fully your spiritual strength and then connect it with your daily activities. Begin looking deeper every day and turn your nice and happy view of life into one that is spectacular and breathtaking.

Too often we are moving around and processing information so quickly, that we don't take enough time to look deeper to reveal the true beauty of the people we are meeting and the work we are doing.

Don't Miss the Opportunity

The sure way to miss success is to miss the opportunity.
— VICTOR CHASLES

After I had taken my seat, an elderly woman boarded the plane. Soon thereafter another man showed up and claimed to be entitled to her seat. The airplane was already full, and there were no other seats left.

It appeared to the man next to me that the airline had made a major mistake. "It looks like the airline issued two boarding passes for the same seat," he said.

So the man and woman began arguing over who had a right to the seat. Several flight attendants intervened. Several minutes went by. The elderly woman got angrier and angrier. She threatened to sue the airline for putting two passengers in the same seat.

Finally, an important-looking airline gate attendant, carrying a walkie talkie, showed up and solved the debate. "Let me see your boarding pass, ma'am," she said. "This flight is not going to Tampa; it is going to Louisville." After all that arguing, it turned out that the elderly woman had boarded the wrong plane and was about to depart for a destination far from the one she desired.

Another example of nearly missing an opportunity because you're heading in the wrong direction was Oprah Winfrey. This celebrated talk show host started out as a television news reporter. For years Oprah tried to fight her way to the top as a television news reporter. She worked hard and put her heart and soul into her job. Oprah made some progress but, finally, the general manager at the television station told her that he wanted her to host a television talk show instead of reporting the news.

Oprah was devastated and vigorously objected to the new assignment. "But I'm a news person," she pleaded in an effort to change the manager's mind. Luckily for her, the pleas did not work. She began hosting the talk show. The audience loved her. Millions of dollars, many years, and an Academy Award later, Oprah Winfrey is not only a successful television star, but she is one of the most recognized celebrity faces in all of America.

We are not always right about the direction we need to head in order to reach our goals. Sometimes, in our passion to reach a goal and make our mark, we begin taking a path that will not take us to our desired destination. In those moments, we become so fixed on reaching a specific goal that we refuse to listen to the advice of others that may lead us to our greatest opportunity for success. We vigorously argue for our place, without stopping to realize that we are on the wrong plane, in the wrong career, or competing in the wrong market.

This week, begin paying closer attention to the people and

events around you in order to make sure you are headed in the right direction. Draw upon your religious faith for the courage and strength to make changes in your life where needed. Give consideration to new opportunities that are presented to you rather than immediately arguing against them. Instead of becoming angry, upset, or depressed when others seem to be taking opportunities that should be going to you, check to make sure that you are even traveling to the destination that will allow you to be successful and to use your talents to the fullest.

We are not always right about the direction we need to head in order to reach our goals. Sometimes, in our passion to reach a goal and make our mark, we begin taking a path that will not take us to our desired destination. In those moments, we become so fixed on reaching a specific goal that we refuse to listen to the advice of others that may lead us to our greatest opportunity for success.

See Things
Differently

Some men see things as they are and ask,
"Why?" I dream things that never were and
ask, "Why not?"
— ROBERT F. KENNEDY

Along the west coast of Ireland, the Cliffs of Moher are an impressive sight. Five miles long and jutting out into the Atlantic Ocean, these four rock formations end at the water's edge by dropping 213 meters (700 feet) nearly straight down into the sea.

My friends walked me to the highest of the four peaks of the cliffs. At the top of this cliff, a small castle had been built. My host MacDara and I marveled at the magnificent view of the Aran Islands on this clear day.

As MacDara and I walked back toward the parking lot, I noticed that some visitors had climbed over the stone fence in order to lie down on the flat rock shelf and to peer over the edge to get a better view. Others went over the fence and to the prior cliff to get a still different view.

As we looked back, we saw a man standing confidently on the flat rock shelf, where others had been lying down to peer over the edge. We noticed that although he appeared to think he was standing upon solid rock, he was actually on a small rock ledge with less than a meter of rock between his feet and the dramatic drop to the ocean below. I wondered how his confident physical posture might change had he been able to see, from my vantage point, what was underneath him.

As leaders, we must be constantly aware that our opinions of what actions to take may change as we change our vantage points. Effective leaders understand this and are constantly on the move. They regularly meet with customers, clients, and constituents to seek their opinions. They visit with employees and volunteers at their places of work to better understand their needs. All of this allows them to constantly see things differently, which is a critical asset in determining a winning direction and guiding a team or organization to success.

This week, think about what you can do differently to see from new vantage points. Although I was looking at the same cliffs that day in Ireland, my appreciation for them changed with nearly every step I took. By endeavoring each day to seek new vantage points in your life, maybe you will begin to dream things the way they can be rather than only seeing things, from your usual position, the way they are.

As leaders, we must be constantly aware that our opinions of what actions to take may change as we change our vantage points. Effective leaders understand this and are constantly on the move. They regularly meet with customers, clients, and constituents to seek their opinions. They visit with employees and volunteers at their places of work to better understand their needs.

IV. Relationship
Management

Freely Give

Freely you have received, freely give.
— MATTHEW 10:8

Among the many people from many countries in the room were the winners of the 2002 Ten Outstanding Young Persons of the World Award presented each year by JCI (Junior Chamber International). Each of the honorees had all overachieved in their young lives but in very different ways.

For example, actress Michelle Yeoh from Malaysia teamed up with Pierce Brosnan in the 1997 James Bond film *Tomorrow Never Dies* and later starred in the award-winning movie *Crouching Tiger, Hidden Dragon.* By contrast, visually impaired Caroline Casey from Ireland trekked 1,000 kilometers across India on the back of an elephant to raise awareness of what people with a disability can do. But despite their varied backgrounds and accomplishments they all had the same answer when speaker Dr. Stephen Covey, author of best-selling books such as *The 7 Habits of Highly Effective*

People, asked a simple question. "If you can recall a time in your life when you were really down and discouraged and someone affirmed or encouraged you in a way that lifted you up and became a turning point in your life, please raise your hand," asked Dr. Covey. Everyone in the room raised a hand.

Throughout the year, people struggle to find the right gifts to present to their loved ones, colleagues, and friends on special occasions that will best express their love, respect, and appreciation. But the greatest gift of all may be to pass along the gift that each of us has received ourselves at critical times in our lives. Often the mere gesture of affirming or encouraging the people around us at the right time and in the right way may have a more lasting and powerful impact than any toy, computer, or piece of jewelry that we might find in a shopping center.

How has your life been changed by someone who encouraged or affirmed you at a difficult or challenging point in your life? As you go throughout each day, do you remember that the recognition of a person's talents, abilities, and skills is in many instances a stronger motivating influence than any tangible compensation? Are you in the habit of freely giving out the same warming and desirable praise that you receive from others?

Most of us, swimming against waves of challenges as we seek as ordinary people to accomplish extraordinary things, only need a little encouragement at the right times to enable us to persevere and achieve our goals. This week, think about giving something to others more valuable and more lasting in impact than money, diamonds, or gold. Freely give encouragement and affirmation to those you love or lead, not only on special occasions, but throughout the year.

Often the mere gesture of affirming or encouraging the people around us at the right time and in the right way may have a more lasting and powerful impact than any toy, computer, or piece of jewelry.

Light the Fire

From the glow of enthusiasm I let the melody escape. I pursue it. Breathless I catch up with it. If flies again, it disappears, it plunges into a chaos of diverse emotions. I catch it again, I seize it, I embrace it with delight.... I multiply it by modulations, and at last I triumph in the first theme. There is the whole symphony.

— LUDWIG VAN BEETHOVEN

A mother should give her children a superabundance of enthusiasm, that after they have lost all they are sure to lose on mixing with the world, enough may still remain to prompt and support them through great actions.

— JULIUS HARE

"Wow! He did it!," my two-year-old son Trevor shouted at the top of his lungs as the wheels of the large airplane touched down on the runway of the airport in Atlanta, Georgia. The other one hundred or so passengers on the plane reacted to Trevor's enthusiastic announcement with laughter and by giving the pilot a round of applause as he finished the landing.

My wife and I did not expect Trevor's reaction to the landing. After being a passenger on fourteen prior flights, we thought that his excitement over an airplane landing would have worn off by now. We expected him to be like the adults on the flight. Rather than acknowledging the really remarkable and important accomplishment of safely landing the plane, most adult passengers usually either ignore the landing or grumble about the slightest rocking of the plane during its approach.

Many of the same events, like the landing of an airplane, which adults might see as ordinary and routine, create excitement and enthusiasm when seen through a child's eyes. Through "mixing with the world" adults lose much of the enthusiasm that caused them as children to celebrate accomplishments and share their excitement more freely.

As business, government, and community leaders, we must continually look for opportunities to celebrate accomplishments to inspire those we lead to show the enthusiasm that will prompt and support them through great actions. Many great achievements throughout history, like the symphonies written by Beethoven, started with the glow of enthusiasm. Without enthusiasm, the creative fire of the team is never lit, and the true potential of the organization is never fully realized.

What are you doing to bring enthusiasm to the team or organization that you lead? Is your team taking for granted routine but important accomplishments rather than appreciating and cel-ebrating them? Do you provide the "glow of enthusiasm" each day that causes others to think, discuss, and ultimately take the actions that will result in your team producing great works?

Trevor's enthusiastic shout inspired a planeful of adults to join him in congratulating the pilot for his routine but important accomplishment. This week, begin looking for routine but impor-tant accomplishments that your team should be celebrating. Make the word "wow!" a part of your everyday vocabulary. Provide "the glow of enthusiasm" that will inspire the team or organization that you lead to achieve great things.

Many great achievements throughout history,
like the symphonies written by Beethoven,
started with the glow of enthusiasm. Without
enthusiasm, the creative fire of the team is never
lit, and the true potential of the organization is
never fully realized.

Believe in
Someone

*To believe in someone is the greatest gift that
you can give.*

— TERRÉ JASPER

My grandmother died in 2003, after fighting off various illnesses and ailments over the previous twenty years of her life. Compared to the many college professors, law school professors, and professional mentors I've had in my life she had very little formal education. But despite that, it was my grandmother who taught me one of the most important tasks of being an outstanding leader.

Over the entire span of my life, my grandmother showed me on a regular basis that she believed in me and that I could accomplish great things. She never once doubted me or my ability. In our many conversations over the years, particularly during the critical teenage years of my life, she kept me grounded in my faith and focused upon doing the right things. Making her proud of me and bringing her joy by seeing me succeed in even the simplest of things have inspired me to always give my best effort and to succeed even as an adult.

Through her unconditional love, unwavering belief, and constant encouragement, my grandmother showed me that the greatest gift you can give isn't something material. The most powerful thing you can give to people, particularly young people, is to show them on a regular basis that you believe in them. She did that for me day after day, during good days and bad, and by doing so, she may have had a greater impact upon what I've been able to accomplish so far in my adult life than perhaps any other person.

What have you done recently to show another person that you believe in him or her? How often do you have meaningful conversations with your young team members, employees, or family members to keep them grounded and focused upon always doing the right thing? Do you enjoy seeing others succeed and show it in a way that inspires them to always give their best efforts and make you proud?

Take a few moments today, and focus on ways to show other people that you believe in them. Effective business, government, community, and family leaders know that nothing is more important in creating long-term and lasting success for your overall team, organization, or family. This week, begin showing other people, especially young people, that you believe in them and, in doing so, give them the greatest gift that you can give to them.

What have you done recently to show another person that you believe in him or her?

Spread Encouraging Words

*Great people are those who make others feel
that they, too, can become great.*
— MARK TWAIN

Stepping off the airplane in southern Brazil, I suddenly remembered an important fact from my early days in school science classes. I learned long ago, but had forgotten, that when the northern hemisphere of the Earth is experiencing summer, the southern hemisphere is experiencing winter. My memory was refreshed by a cold wind blowing in my face and seeing my breath as I exhaled.

Hours earlier, I had left the sweltering summertime heat of my home in Kentucky. Not thinking about the difference in weather patterns between the two hemispheres, I had arrived in Brazil without an overcoat. Discovering my dilemma, my colleague Jun quickly took off his own overcoat and insisted that I wear it. Jun wanted me to stay warm even if it meant he would be cold himself.

Jun's offering of his coat to me was not only appreciated, but it was an example of how great leaders guide with encouraging actions as well as words. Outstanding business, government, community, and family leaders selflessly make others feel as though they can become great even if it means forgoing their own opportunity or benefit. They are willing to make others feel warm with no expectation that the warmth will be returned. They constantly affirm those around them, even though it might take considerable energy and time to do so.

How have you been sharing encouragement with others? When you think of something nice to say about an employee, colleague, or team member, do you take the time and energy to write it down, or do you let those thoughts drift from your mind without ever passing them on? Are you willing to affirm and support others when doing so might mean sacrificing an opportunity or benefit for yourself?

This week, think about what strategies you might follow to more effectively recognize and inspire others. Look for talent, ability, and potential in every person you meet and give those people sincere compliments generously and selflessly. Achieve greatness as a leader by doing all you can possibly do to make others feel that they, too, can become great.

Leaders are willing to make others feel warm with no expectation that the warmth will be returned. They constantly affirm those around them, even though it might take considerable energy and time to do so.

See More Stars

*Leaders often forget that people arrive on the
scene predisposed to do a good job. I'm
always impressed with the films—they are
invariably terrible films—in which the young
player rushes up and says, "Send me in,
Coach." People are hard-wired to want
to be sent in.*

— LIONEL TIGER

At 4:30 a.m. our van was winding its way to the
top of Mount Haleakala on the Hawaiian island of Maui. Mount
Haleakala, over 10,000 feet (3,048 meters) in elevation above sea
level, is the largest dormant volcano in the world.

We were making our way to the top of Haleakala to catch the
dramatic sunrise from its crest and then to descend on bicycles
the thirty-eight miles (sixty-one kilometers) down the volcano to
the ocean. The sunrise and the bicycle ride were supposed to

leave the biggest impressions on me that day, but they didn't. What impressed me the most that day was the pre-dawn sky.

Far from any large city and high above sea level, I was able to see thousands more stars from the top of Haleakala than I can see on the clearest nights at my home in Kentucky. Even though it is the same sky I look at in Kentucky, the increased elevation and the remote location of the Hawaiian Islands allowed me to see the night sky differently.

Being able to see things differently is an important trait of outstanding business, government, and community leaders. Just as I was able to see the night sky differently by changing location, outstanding leaders are able to get a clearer view of their organizations by elevating their own thinking and removing themselves from distractions. As a result, they put themselves in a position to look at the individuals on their team and see more "stars." When they look at their team members, they see abilities, possibilities, and talents that less-focused leaders overlook. These outstanding leaders work hard to get the best performance out of all individuals and not just a selected few.

How many stars do you see when you look at your team? Do you lead each day with an understanding that everyone on your team has a natural desire to do a good job and achieve? Are you trying too hard to create stars, when all you really need to do is help the stars you already have to shine?

This week, take a closer look at every member on your team. Remember that those you lead "arrive on the scene predisposed to do a good job." Make an effort to see more stars, and both you and your organization will be more successful.

Outstanding leaders are able to get a clearer view of their organizations by elevating their own thinking and removing themselves from distractions. As a result, they put themselves in a position to look at the individuals on their team and see more "stars."

Show a Little Respect

Respect a man, he will do more.
— James Howell

He that respects not is not respected.
— George Hebert

"Say 'yes, sir' to the nice gentleman," I told my young son, trying to instill in him some basic manners. Thinking that parents can help children succeed by teaching them manners reminded me of the great impact that showing respect to others can have on my own success as an adult.

Examining my own actions, I have found that I don't always show others as much respect as I should. I too often let my emotions, enthusiasm, and stress control my initial contact with people, rather than pausing to address them first in a polite,

179

mannerly, and respectful way.

Outstanding leaders understand that simply showing respect as you greet someone is an effective way to break the ice. Creating a good feeling at the outset helps leaders get their points across. They know they will get better results, even from difficult conversations, if they show others respect from the start.

How do you greet others before you begin a conversation or meeting? Do your initial words and gestures acknowledge others and show them that they are important to you and that you value the opportunity to meet them? Are you always positive and uplifting at the beginning of a conversation or dialogue, even when you expect the eventual discussion to be difficult?

This week, show more respect to others when you greet them. Through your initial words, demonstrate to them that you value and appreciate the opportunity to work with them. Earn respect from others by first showing your respect for them.

Simply showing respect as you greet someone is an effective way to break the ice. Creating a good feeling at the outset helps leaders get their points across. They know they will get better results, even from difficult conversations, if they show others respect from the start.

Boost Their
Self-Esteem

*Outstanding leaders go out of their way to
boost the self-esteem of their personnel. If
people believe in themselves, it's amazing
what they can accomplish.*
— SAM WALTON

In the Golden Globe Award winning movie, *As
Good as it Gets,* Melvin, played by Jack Nicholson, is a successful
novelist but also an obsessive-compulsive man with the meanest
mouth in Manhattan. Somehow Melvin arranges dinner with a
nice but financially struggling waitress named Carol. As they enter the restaurant, the host tells Melvin that they cannot be seated
unless Melvin is wearing a coat and tie. Surprised by this, Melvin
asks Carol to wait for him while he leaves to find a coat and tie.

When Melvin returns to the restaurant, Carol compliments

him as to how nice the coat and tie look on him. But in thanking her, Melvin proceeds to explain that he really could not believe they would insist upon him wearing a coat and tie when they allowed her to enter wearing a "simple house dress." Insulted, Carol rises from her chair and threatens to leave if Melvin does not give her a compliment immediately. He replies by telling her that he is taking his medicine again.

Not satisfied, Carol turns to leave. Melvin stops her and explains that he is supposed to take medicine to help him control his behavior and that he started taking it again when they first met. Carol asks Melvin to get to the point. He then says, "You make me want to be a better man."

Carol melts back into her seat and responds, "That is the nicest thing anyone has ever said to me."

Organizations and teams can only achieve greatness when their members, who may feel capable of only ordinary efforts, are encouraged to work together to give an extraordinary effort every day. And these team members only give such an effort when leaders like you show them how extraordinary they can be. Only then do they go about their work with commitment, energy, and enthusiasm.

The ultimate force you can create to move your team and organization toward greatness is to inspire each person in your organization to become an exceptional human being and not just a good employee, partner, or volunteer. You must earn a high level of respect from them by doing more than just going through the usual motions of a manager. You must find a way to win the hearts, as well as the minds, of those you lead by taking a genuine interest in them as individuals.

Do you take time out of your busy daily schedule to encourage those working hard for your team? Is your mind completely focused on the person in your organization that comes to you asking for help, or are you thinking ahead to your next phone call or next appointment? Do you take the opportunity, whenever individuals excel in their assigned duties, to praise them in a way that boosts their self-esteem and causes them to believe in themselves?

As a leader, you can have a powerful impact on individuals and your organization by inspiring them rather than merely managing them. Carol was unaware of the awesome power she held to inspire Melvin to want to become a better man. This week, go out of your way to boost the self-esteem of those you lead. Motivate them to be more than just good team members. Encourage them to believe in themselves and to feel they can become outstanding men and women.

Organizations and teams can only achieve greatness when their members, who may feel capable of only ordinary efforts, are encouraged to work together to give an extraordinary effort every day.

Accept
Criticism

To avoid criticism, do nothing, say nothing,
be nothing.

— ELBERT HUBBARD

As I began my exercise walk early in the morning along Miami Beach, I passed a motor home. Inside the motor home, a young fashion model was having her make-up applied as a crew began preparing for a photography shoot. From a music system on the motor home, I could hear the reggae version of the song "Red, Red Wine," first written and recorded by Neil Diamond many years ago.

Today, Neil Diamond's songs have been re-recorded by many groups from rock bands to reggae bands. His music has played a key role in scenes in popular movies such as *Pulp Fiction*. Thirty years after he first performed them, his songs have stood the test of time.

Neil Diamond's songs were not always so widely appreciated. Although he had a loyal following, the songs that he wrote and sang in the 1970s were often the subject of ridicule and the brunt of jokes. Music critics generally hated everything that he created.

No one can expect to create anything that has an impact without being criticized by at least a few people. But great business, government, and community leaders do not let criticism keep them from accomplishing things that will allow them to leave their mark on other individuals, their team, and the world.

Think of ways this week that you can remind yourself each day that criticism is just a natural response to a leader who is making great things happen. If you can learn to tolerate criticism, no matter how intense and vicious, as Diamond did, then you can be a leader that does and says things that have a deep impact on people for years to come.

No one can expect to create anything that has an impact without being criticized by at least a few people. But great leaders do not let criticism keep them from accomplishing things that will allow them to leave their mark on other individuals, their team, and the world.

Give What
You Have

*Give what you have. To someone it may be
better than you dare to think.*
— Henry Wadsworth Longfellow

While in a remote area in West Africa, I bent
over the bathtub in my hotel room to turn the water on and take
a shower. But even though I twisted the knob as far as I could,
nothing came out. After about a minute of waiting, brown water
slowly began trickling out. Eventually the water became clearer,
but there was not enough pressure to make the water come out of
the shower head.

Resigning myself to just leaning over the edge of the bathtub
to wash my hair, I cupped my hands, rinsed my hair, and then
lathered it up with shampoo. Just as I was getting ready to rinse
out the shampoo, the water suddenly stopped flowing. Now I

had a major problem!

I waited several minutes for the water to come back, but nothing happened. I looked around for alternatives. The only thing I could see was a small amount of water in the bottom of the toilet basin.

Then, fortunately, I remembered a small gift that I had received from my hosts the night before: a large bottle of drinking water that I had not completely consumed. Retrieving the bottle from my nightstand, I found just enough water remaining in that bottle to completely rinse the shampoo out of my hair and to save the day.

The bottle of drinking water did not seem like much of a gift at the time I received it. But without it, I would have been in very difficult circumstances. With a full day of business activities ahead of me, a sticky and slimy head of hair would have made a poor impression. That simple bottle of water was more important to me than my hosts could have imagined.

Throughout the year and particularly during the holiday season, it may sometimes seem that what we have to give to others is not large, expensive, or impressive enough. What we are able to give might seem simple and insignificant when we compare it to what we see others giving or what we are receiving. But as my bottle of water proved that day in Africa, we never know what great value others may find in gifts we believe are very simple. What matters most is to make a habit of always giving what we have and giving it generously.

This week, remember that what you give—be it a tangible item, your skills, your talents, or simply your attention—may have more value to others than you realize. Don't strive to always give the largest, most impressive, or most expensive gift. Just give what you have. Remember that what you have, even if you don't think it is good enough, may be a greater gift than you dare imagine.

We never know what great value others may find in gifts we believe are very simple. What matters most is to make a habit of always giving what we have and giving it generously.